BARCELONA
AND SITGES

BARCELONA
AND SITGES

By Paul Clements

Published by Thomas Cook Publishing
A division of Thomas Cook Tour Operations Limited
Company Registration No.1450464 England.
The Thomas Cook Business Park, Coningsby Road
Peterborough PE3 8SB, United Kingdom
email: books@thomascook.com
www.thomascookpublishing.com
+ 44 (0) 1733 416477

ISBN-13: 978-1-84157-662-6
ISBN-10: 1-84157-662-X

First edition © 2003 Thomas Cook Publishing
Second edition © 2006
Text © 2006 Thomas Cook Publishing
Maps © 2006 Thomas Cook Publishing
Transport map © 2006 Communicarta Ltd

Written by Paul Clements
Updated by Warwick Worldwide

Original photography by Gavin Harrison

Additional photography:
A1 Pix: pages 58, 66 and 101
Alamy Images: page 33
FOTOLIA – page 25 © Trevor Allen; page 83 © Photosmart;
page 95 © Dragan Trifunovic; page 138 © rachel Collinson
Hotel Axel: page 124
Pictures Colour Library: page 51
Neil Setchfield: page 116
Spectrum Colour Library: page 119

Front cover photography © Alamy Images

Design and layout: 183 Books, Thorney, Peterborough and Grassverge

Project Editor: Linda Bass
Production/DTP: Steven Collins

Printed and bound in Italy by Printer Trento

Contents

CONTENTS

My Kind of Town...

I've been in love with Barcelona since my university days when my Catalan roommate gave me an exhaustive tour of his home town. On subsequent return trips I have hung out in the city's gay bars, practising chat-up lines in broken Spanish with surprising success. In my book, that's reason enough to love a place and its people.

Travelling is not only a passion, it's my job. As deputy editor of British Airways' glossy magazine, *High Life*, I get to see the world – though Barcelona remains my favourite city by a long lead. When not sitting cross-legged in a Tokyo tofu restaurant, haring around the neighbourhoods of Santiago de Chile (another favourite city), or in New York interviewing the likes of Mariah Carey and Tom Jones in their hotel suites, I also write a monthly city guide for *Business Life*. So I get around.

I have been the guest 'travel-shooter' on BBC Radio 1's *Sunday Surgery* phone-in show and hosted the station's annual travel week webchat. I am also the author of *Out Around London*, another guidebook in this series.

Equally relevant to my credentials is that I have been the longest serving editor of *The Pink Paper*, Britain's lesbian and gay newspaper. I took up this position at the age of 21, which made me the youngest editor of a national title. After that, and despite by then being something of a professional homosexual, I was invited to join the *Mail on Sunday* to work on the entertainment and news review, *Night&Day*. My next career move will, I hope, involve relocation to Barcelona.

But until I've mastered the local languages (plural) and found that perfect apartment in the Eixample, or something in Poble Nou with a sea view, you'll find me propping up the city's bars every few months. When in Barça, mine's a *vodka limón*. Do come and say *hola*.

Barcelona shore

Out in Barcelona

Barcelona has made many names for itself since hosting the Olympic Games in 1992, a defining moment in its 2,000-year history. Today, it is known the world over as a design city, a party town, a gastro capital, and a gay magnet – the unquestionable jewel of the Mediterranean. Call it what you will, when it comes to names, names, names, Barcelona is a label queen.

What Barcelona's got, she flaunts. And you name it, she's got it. Spain's second city is cradled between the last gasp of the Pyrenees and the shores of the Mediterranean, and is blessed with sun, sea, sand and sexy people in every direction. Mere minutes from the city centre, its beaches are perfect for a cooling dip in summer (if there's space), or for an afternoon sashay in winter. And, 20 minutes down the Costa Dorada, there's the truly wonderful town of Sitges. This former fishing port is, after Ibiza, Europe's gayest beach playground. You'll find a mini guide to Sitges starting on page 99.

Finding your way in Barcelona is as easy as finding things to see and to do. The city is neatly divided into 'uptown' and 'downtown' by Plaça de Catalunya – the huge historic central square with fountains and benches where idlers come to mill and tourists come to twirl in awe as they get their bearings. Although never referred to as such, uptown is the Eixample (or 'expansion') which filthy rich Catalans, tired of being confined to the brimming gothic city, colonised in the late 19th century. They commissioned grand homes from leading architects of the movement known as Modernisme – a Catalan take on Art Nouveau and not to be confused with what is known elsewhere as Modernism. Guess which community flocked to resurrect this architecturally flamboyant district after dictator Franco allowed it to go to seed?

Most famous of all Modernista architects is Antonio Gaudí, whose creations have become landmarks of Barcelona. His most cherished and emblematic work is the Sagrada Família, an unfinished cathedral with soaring towers and fantastical façades depicting scenes from the Bible in rapturous detail.

Down from Plaça de Catalunya is the cobbled labyrinth of the Old City, whose streets date back to the 13th century. These passageways are as narrow and gnarled as they are absorbing, a world away from the Eixample, and filled with little shops and unexpected squares, bustling cafés and bars. The old quarter (Barri Gòtic), home to Barcelona's other cathedral, the romanesque masterpiece La Seu, is separated from the once seedy but now scrubbed up Raval area by the city's most famous address, La Rambla: a mile-long café-strewn avenue which literally paves the way to the Mediterranean.

At its foot is the Old Port (Port Vell). Thanks to extensive renovations completed for the Olympic Games, this is actually new, and now the largest working port in Europe. Then there are the beaches of Barceloneta, which stretch for miles along the coast, again belatedly cleaned up to provide a suitably stunning backdrop for the Olympic Village (Vila Olímpic). Mar Bella, an accessible nudist beach around 30 minutes' stroll from Barceloneta metro station, is where the gays are.

In the opposite direction from the port is Montjuïc, a craggy, 200m-high outpost that's home to the stadiums and sporting arenas which hosted the Olympic Games, as well as a bevy of museums, galleries and leafy walkways left over from the much-vaunted International Exhibition, held there in 1929.

So where should you begin? Most newcomers start with La Rambla. Indeed, it would be hard to avoid this street which has been Barcelona's backbone since it was paved and turned into a boulevard in the late 18th century. It is a feast for the senses and a suitable place to take the city's temperature – which is invariably hot, with a racing pulse.

Here, you'll also get a feel for kinks in the social fabric, which is by turns oh-so elegant and grungily bohemian. Veer off La Rambla – with its glitzy department stores at the top and seedier flavour at the other end – and head deeper into the Old City. The chances are you will either find *granja* milk bars full of well-to-do society ladies gossiping in brisk

Catalan and sipping *xocolata* (hot chocolate), or you will bump into edgy characters (beggars, drug addicts and transvestite prostitutes) seemingly in search of a Pedro Almodóvar film. That is half the attraction of Barcelona. She is a diva.

As with every diva, there is hidden sadness here. She is a city masking a painful past. Barcelona is the capital of Catalonia (Catalunya), a semi-autonomous region in the north-east of the Iberian peninsula which has for centuries been fighting to achieve independence from Madrid.

And mind your language here. Barcelona is not Spanish. In this bilingual city the mother tongue is Catalan, a thriving romance language spoken by over 7 million people (and not just inside Catalonia's borders, but in neighbouring France and Andorra, too). This language not only has much in common with Castillian Spanish, but fizzes between the teeth and sounds – say some – like a drunk Spaniard attempting French. Everywhere in Barcelona the pecking order is clear: Catalan first, Castillian second. Although both languages have equal legal status, all street signs are in Catalan, as are many menus, and tourists receive an extra warm smile if they greet shopkeepers with a tentative 'Bon dia' (Catalan for hello) instead of 'Buenos dias'. A few useful expressions are included on pages 144–145.

But what about the gay scene? Homosexuality was decriminalised in Spain in 1822 and the age of consent was brought down to 12 years of age for both heterosexuals and homosexuals in 1996. Two years later, the Catalan government proved its liberal mettle by recognising gay partnerships in law, a move since repeated across Spain, with very little opposition, by the socialist government. Barcelona has long been at the gay vanguard, championing Spain's first Pride event in 1977. It now alternates as host for the national gay day with Madrid, when scene mavens in both cities can be bothered to organise one. (See p.89.)

Human statues

In terms of a gay village, Barcelona's is the gridded quarter in the left Eixample, north of Gran Via, between Comte d'Urgell and Aribau – and commonly referred to as the 'Gaixample' (gay-zhyam-pluh). A quick stroll along Consell de Cent, Diputació, Casanova and Muntaner reveals a concentration of gay bars, clubs and shops. Gay men and lesbians mix well here and both are welcome in each other's bars. There is even one men-only sleaze joint, Martins (see p.82), which has a big transgender following, especially with those with pneumatic busts. But broadly speaking the Eixample is boyztown. If the girls want to be alone they head to Gràcia, the well-heeled neighbourhood north of Avinguda Diagonal – or to Sitges or Figueres, some 100 kilometres north, where there's a burgeoning lesbian population. (See p.115.)

For all its similarities with world-class destinations like London, New York and Sydney, Barcelona is not a 24-hour city. Most shops close for three hours in the afternoon for a siesta – an old-fashioned concept these days. But you'll be grateful for the nap, as bars stay open until the last person leaves. Here, getting home as the sun comes up is considered reasonable behaviour.

Barcelona has a rhythm, which translates on the gay scene into a strict routine. Bars fill and empty with quartz-like precision. A night out begins comparatively late and certainly never before 11pm, when the bars are still empty. Start at Punto for drinks, then at midnight head to Dietrich or Z:eltas for a spot of dancing and mingling. Then at 3am, it's on to your club of choice. After that, there's always an after-hours club to be found (ask any cloakroom or door attendant for flyers). Similarly, if it's sauna fun that you are after, they tend to get busy during the siesta. Going out with gay friends requires synchronised watches.

People here are very interested in checking each other out, so dress to impress. Even the smallest and quietest neighbourhood bar won't just have a resident DJ but a resident drag act, too. During the course of a night expect the lights to be dimmed and a space to be cleared for an immaculately turned out female impersonator (or, in classier places, a post-op transsexual) to lip synch her way through some full-lunged power ballad.

But that's quintessential Barcelona. What can you do except applaud wildly and shout 'Viva la diva!'

Sagrada sculpture

Stepping Out

When in Barcelona, you don't need a checklist of sights. There is plenty to marvel at all around. But there is a handful of remarkable attractions – from instantly recognisable Gaudí landmarks to the unique minimalist summer pavilion hidden at the foot of Montjuïc – that will enrich your stay.

For all its treasures, Barcelona is a compact city that gives up its gems easily. Take them in aboard one of the many tour buses, or better still by simply walking around. The city is relatively flat and it pays to dive down alleyways that take your fancy. You are unlikely to wander too far from a metro station and are more likely to find a charming church, square or café to call your own.

My Top Sights

La Sagrada Família

Honeycomb spires

ⓘ Entrances on C. Sardenya and C. Mallorca 📞 93 207 30 31 www.sagradafamilia.org 🕐 Oct–Mar daily 9am–6pm; April–Sept daily 9am–8pm 🚇 Metro: Sagrada Família. Bus 19, 33, 34, 43, 44, 50, 51 🎟 €8; Passion tower lift €2

Antonio Gaudí's Sagrada Família is the most flamboyant cathedral of the modern age. Engulfing a whole block of the Eixample like a monolithic sandcastle, its dizzying honeycomb spires look like dripping wax, while its colourful sculpted façades animate the Bible story in passionate detail. It is also Barcelona's most popular attraction, pulling in more than a million slack-jawed visitors a year. Not bad for what is essentially a building site.

STEPPING OUT

The sheer scale of this visionary benchmark of modern religious architecture is breathtaking. Once the tallest building in the city, its spires reach almost 100m into the air and are coloured with ornate mosaics and decorations inspired by nature. Instead of ugly gothic gargoyles, there are doves, serpents, turtles, and even a life-size donkey. Those on either side of the nave depict the Nativity and Passion; the craggily magnificent main entrance is topped by the Glory façade. It is small wonder that Jean Cocteau called the cathedral 'a mindscraper'.

A tour should include a peek inside the newly completed nave with its tree-like stone supports, the cloister, and the vaulted chamber that will eventually support the centrepiece tower representing Christ, yet to be built. A team of international architects is now racing to finish the thing for 2026, the centenary of Gaudí's death.

Parc Güell

ℹ️ C. d'Olot ☀️ 10am–dusk daily Ⓜ️ Metro: Lesseps. Bus 24, 25. Bus Turístic to the gate 🎫 Free

Parc Güell is one of Barcelona's most enchanting open spaces, a surreal wonderland of sloping terraces, fairytale pavilions and hidden recesses.

Set in forest land on a steep hill overlooking downtown, with fantastic views over the whole city, the ambitious project was completed (by Gaudí) in 1914. It features a riot of *trencadís* tiling – a decorative technique pioneered by Gaudí using broken glass and ceramic to give sculptures a hardwearing but colourful mosaic coat – and is full of the architect's characteristically fanciful features and naturalistic exuberance. There is the Sala Hipóstila, originally intended as a market hall, a grand staircase 'guarded' by a mosaic salamander, a winding ceramic bench picked out with *trencadís*.

Gaudí was keen on puzzles and

Remarkable roofs

opaque symbolism. Here you'll find a hermetically sealed chapel (no one has ever worked out how to get in), a maze-like network of rambling paths and viaducts, and the Torre Rosa, the architect's former home which is now a small, shrine-like museum, the Casa-Museu Gaudí.

Casa-Museu Gaudí

ℹ️ Inside Park Güell, C. de Carmen
📞 93 284 64 46
☀️ Mar–Apr 10am–7pm; May–Sept 10am–8pm; Oct–Feb 10am–6pm 🎫 €3

Boqueria market

La Rambla

🚇 Metro: Catalunya, Liceu, Drassanes

No trip to Barcelona would be complete without a stroll along its most celebrated street. Running from Plaça de Catalunya all the way to the rejuvenated port, all roads seem to lead to this wide, leafy, part-pedestrianised avenue, which to the gay poet Lorca was the most beautiful in the world. Although much of La Rambla's 19th-century charm has worn off – until the pre-1992 clean-up it had been a particularly dangerous red-light district – it is still home to some of the city's most charming landmarks. These include the Boqueria market, the Liceu opera house and the Font de las Canaletes – a fountain from which, legend has it, every tourist must drink in order to ensure a safe return to the city. There's also a pavement mosaic by Miró and a variety of churches to be taken in.

But the greatest pleasure to be had along this kilometre-long drag is the walk itself. An artery of theatricality, La Rambla throbs with life at all times of the day and night. (See pp.29–35.)

Catedral de Barcelona (La Seu)

ℹ️ Plaça de la Seu 📞 93 342 82 60 ✴️ Mon–Sat 1.15pm–4.30pm; Sun 2pm–5.15 pm 🚇 Metro: Jaume I. Bus 17, 19, 40, 45 🎟️ €4

An antidote to Barcelona's more famous cathedral (see p.13), the gothic masterpiece of La Seu is – unlike Gaudí's half-finished effort – in full working order as the city's spiritual bedrock.

Built in 1298 on the site of a former Roman temple that was later occupied by two churches (a 4th-century baptistery destroyed by maurauding Moors and a replacement Romanesque basilica), it wasn't finished until 150 years later, in 1448 – a familiar story in Barcelona. Even then, it had to make do without a western-facing main façade overlooking Plaça Nova for another four centuries. Seeing it floodlit at night is enough to convince anyone that it was worth the wait.

The finished La Seu was finally unveiled in 1888 when finances permitted the façade's construction using plans dating back to the 15th century. Consequently, it is a mishmash of Gothic style and neo-Gothic stylings, with Baroque and Romanesque chapels, Renaissance screens and Modernista stained-glass windows. Thrillseekers will be more interested in the lift that whisks visitors to the roof for superb views across the Barri Gòtic.

But there's plenty to be seen inside. Don't miss the low-slung crypt containing the alabaster sarcophagus of Santa Eulàlia, a patroness of Barcelona whose

The old cathedral

breasts were sliced off by the Romans during one of 13 grisly torture sessions prior to her crucifixion.

Yet the most popular and fanciful part is the 14th-century cloister, with a shady, palm-fronded garden at its centre, home to a family of honking geese which has been there for five centuries. Perhaps the best time to visit is Sunday morning, when the cathedral provides an imposing backdrop for groups of mostly elderly dancers in the Plaça de la Seu performing the *sardana*, a local hotstep which is surprisingly fiendish to pull off.

Fundació Joan Miró

ⓘ A. l'Estadi, Parc de Montjuic
📞 93 443 94 70   www.bcn.fjmiro.es
🚇 Metro: Paral-lel (then funicular), or Espanya then up the escalators. Bus 50, 55
🕐 Oct–Jun Tues, Wed, Fri, Sat 10am–7pm; Thur 10am–9.30pm; Sun 10am–2.30pm; Jul–Sept Tues, Wed, Fri, Sat 10am–8pm; Thur 10am–9.30pm; Sun 10am–2.30pm 💶 All exhibitions €7.50, €5 concessions. Permanent collection only €4, €3 concessions

Barcelona has two world-class museums devoted to two masters of modern art: Pablo Picasso and Joan Miró, both of whom worked extensively in the city. While the Picasso Museum contains no truly major pieces, the Fundació Joan Miró houses the most comprehensive selection of its namesake's work anywhere in the world. Take an audioguide, or a guided tour in English – or plot your own route through his colourful career (pun intended).

Housed in a splendid white building on Montjuïc, specially built in 1975 by his friend Josep Lluís Sert, the collection of more than 400 paintings and sculptures opens with a remarkable room of tapestries. After an exploration of his younger works, it's on to the real meat: the best of his Cubist and Surrealist periods. Highlights include the set of 50 lithographs completed after the Civil War, called *Barcelona Series*. On top of the building is a quiet sculpture terrace, with Miró's playful 3D works.

Of all the intriguing non-Miró pieces here, most popular is the mesmerising mercury fountain by Alexander Calder, first exhibited in 1937 alongside Picasso's *Guernica*.

Even for non-art fans, the Fundació is a great excuse to ride the funicular from Paral-lel metro (see p.51), and there's a decent café, too.

Fundació Joan Miró

Montjuïc

🔵 Espanya. Funicular from Paral·lel. Bus 50 and others from Plaça d'Espanya

Montjuïc – the hilly parkland rising up beside the port – means 'Jewish mountain' in Catalan. It is known today to Barcelonans as 'pink mountain', not least because its bushes are full of gay men pretending to walk their dogs in the thicket, or around the Teatre Grec amphitheatre, regardless of the time of day or weather.

Its prime interest, however, is as a historical location for some spectacular sporting events and artistic landmarks. It was here that much of the 1992 Olympic Games were played out, in the Estadi Olímpic and the swimming lanes of the Piscines Bernat Picornell, which are open to the public (see p.97). Visually, the Anella Olímpic's crowning glory is the Torre Calatrava, a ghost-white looped mast that dominates the Plaça Sant Jordi and also doubles as a giant sundial.

Art fans will appreciate the Fundació Joan Miró (see opposite); the spectacular Museu Nacional d'Art de Catalunya inside the Palau Nacional (see pp.45,48); the recreated Pavelló Barcelona, and German architect Mies van der Rohe's marble and onyx pavilion.

Olympic pool

Parc de la Ciutadella

ℹ️ Passeig Picasso 🌗 Sunrise–sunset daily 🔵 Metro: Arc de Triomf, Barceloneta. Bus 14, 39, 40, 42, 51, 100, 541 💲 Free

What this park between La Ribera and the Vila Olímpic lacks in looks, it more than makes up for in history and folkloric attractions. Steeped in incident, it was originally a citadel torn into the heart of La Ribera by the king's troops after the 1714 siege of Barcelona so that they could train their cannons on the unruly Catalan city from within. In later, more settled years, it was converted into a 150-acre public park (and in 1888 hosted the Universal Exhibition, at which Modernisme was unveiled to the wider world).

Today, it's a busy recreational and educational park where families come for mind-broadening day trips, and the style brigade from the nearby Born district come to stretch their legs during the siesta. Its highlights include the zoo, the Museu d'Art Modern (which currently shares premises with the Catalan Parliament), and the impressive Modernista brick edifice of the Museu de Zoologia. There's also low-key cruising to be had around the Cascadas, a grandiose fountain-cum-monument.

Architectural lines

Pavelló Barcelona

🛈 A. Marquès de Comillas
📞 93 423 40 16 www.miesbcn.com
🕙 10am–8pm daily Ⓜ Metro: Espanya.
Bus 13, 50 Ⓥ €3.50

Of all the museums and attractions on Montjuïc, perhaps the most intriguing – and certainly the one with the fewest exhibits – is this sleek summer pavilion. Conceived by genius German designer Ludwig Mies van der Rohe, who made famous the mantra 'less is more', the cool one-storey construction is a landmark of rationalist architecture. It will thrill anyone who's ever drooled over a copy of *Wallpaper* magazine.

A boxy structure built from onyx, chrome and glass, with no definite purpose other than to 'enclose space' (as one of Mies van der Rohe's contemporaries swooned) and blur the boundary between outdoors and indoors, its clean lines were revolutionary when unveiled, the German entry to Barcelona's 1929 International Exhibition.

There's little to see inside – this is architecture for architecture's sake after all, although the on-site shop has the trendiest general Barcelona postcards in town.

Passeig de Gràcia

Ⓜ Metro: Plaça de Catalunya,
Passeig de Gràcia, Diagonal.
Bus: 17, 24, 28, the Tom bús

Barcelona's other great avenue (after La Rambla), this broad, plane-tree-lined boulevard is famed as much today for its shopping as for its extraordinary concentration of Modernista architecture. To walk along it from Plaça de Catalunya is to pass some of the most important works of the period – mostly mansion blocks commissioned by the city's status-aware citizens in the late-19th century.

But look up above the shop fronts and you'll drop your bags in awe. Within a few blocks along this one street there's La Pedrera, a cream cake of a building (by Gaudí, naturally) with undulating windows and balconies and not a straight line in sight; Casa Batlló, Gaudí's rippling dragon house, now open to visitors for the first time; and Casa Amatller, a quite different mansion house altogether, built for a chocolate magnate and looking like a gingerbread house.

The rippling dragon house

Boats at Port Vell

The beaches

 Metro: Barceloneta, Ciutadella Vila Olímpica, Bogatell, Poble Nou (for Mar Bella). Bus: 36, 41

Thanks to the 1992 Olympics, Barcelona now has some of the best inner-city beaches in Europe, which are walking distance from the bottom of La Rambla. This being a city built on looks, even the concrete sunloungers at Platja Nova Icària are works of art.

The westernmost point of interest is Port Vell (Old Port), Barcelona's innermost working harbour with an imposing (but uninspiring) darkened glass shopping complex, Maremàgnum, the city's aquarium and an Imax cinema. Rather than bother with air-conditioned precincts, tread the Rambla del Mar instead, a wavy boardwalk that rotates to let boats pass, and admire pop artist Roy Lichtenstein's mosaic sculpture, *Barcelona Head*, on Moll de la Fusta. Here you can also hire a catamaran to tour the harbour. (See p.57.)

Heading east on foot is beachy Barceloneta. Its *platjas* stretch for several kilometres from Sant Sebastià (where you can take the precarious and expensive cable car to Montjuïc – see p.51), so pack a swimming costume – or head a couple of kilometres past the Port Olímpic to Mar Bella, the nudist section popular with gays. If it's water sports you're after, there's a hire centre here.

On the way is Port Olímpic, a haven for rollerbladers and gentle cyclists (for hire details – see pp.96–97).

Heavenly spires

Around Town

Barcelona began life as Barcino, a cramped walled Roman city – remnants of which can still be seen around the Barri Gòtic, Europe's largest medieval neighbourhood – before busting its seams intermittently to form overspill neighbourhoods. So, in the mid-1700s Barceloneta was built on reclaimed land around the harbour. The Eixample sprang up on former farmland in 1854, after Madrid conceded that the Bourbon walls causing chronic overcrowding in La Ribera could be torn down. Montjuïc was landscaped in 1914 to provide green space and a lofty platform to house the city's art collections, museums and (latterly) its conference halls. Most recently, in the mid-1980s came the transformation of the grotty industrial port into a waterside playground. Consequently, Barcelona has been bequeathed a handful of distinct quarters, each a specific time capsule of history and architecture, with its own look and feel, and each detailed in the coming chapters.

The Eixample

Split into a left (Esquerra de l'Eixample) and a right (Dreta de l'Eixample) quarter, which divide along a former tram line at C. de Balmes, the Eixample was colonised by Gaudí and lesser-known (though no less important) contemporaries like Lluís Domènech i Montaner and Puig i Cadafalch. While the area's biggest tourist draw remains the Sagrada Família and the shops along the Passeig de Gràcia (many of which occupy stunning Modernista landmarks), the streets themselves are a fantastical wonderland of grandiose set pieces. These include Casa Amatller, splashed with pink and burgundy ceramics; Casa Milà (the cream cake-like La Pedrera); Casa de les Puntxes (or House of Spikes); and the world's only UNESCO-protected hospital, Santa Creu i Sant Pau by Domènech i Montaner. Even the humblest corner pharmacies from the period retain their ornate shop signs with stylistic flourishes, and the stone street benches

which support magnificent wrought-iron lampposts betray lusty Modernista stylings.

Of the two, the Left Eixample is the poorer relation – it has its share of visual frippery but less by way of must-see attractions – but it happens to be where gay life came to flourish, post-Franco. Now home to the city's village, it has earned the nickname of the Gaixample. *(See p.25.)*

A DAY OUT

Given the size of the Eixample, which stretches from C. Tarragona and Sants train station to C. Independència and the decidedly unlovely Plaça Glòries Catalanes roundabout, it's advisable to set aside the best part of a day to see its major sights. That said – and despite the quarter's gentle uphill incline (when facing away from the sea) – it is eminently walkable.

Our walking tour starts in Plaça de Catalunya at the foot of Passeig de Gràcia, Eixample's swanky shopping belt. This is home to some of the most noteworthy Modernista landmarks the city has to offer, with dazzling creations paving every step of the way. The first major point of interest is the block known as the Mansana de la Discòrdia. Between C. Consell de Cent (Barcelona's answer to London's Old Compton Street) and C. d'Aragó is the 'block of discord', so called because each *casa* was built to outshine the next in sheer ostentation. First up is Casa Lleó Morera, a once spectacular residential block by Domènech i Montaner, which was later ruined at street level by a shop-front conversion. At No. 41 is Casa Amatller, Josep Puig i Cadafalch's ceramic-stippled fairytale hideaway, topped off by a stepped pyramid façade. Entry is restricted to the lobby and the first floor but here you can get further information about the movement and its landmarks, as well as free guided tours of the Mansana de la Discòrdia, from the Centre del Modernisme housed here.

The most impressive sight along the Mansana de la Discòrdia (though, legend has it, the beholder has to decide) is Gaudí's offering, Casa Battló, a so-so townhouse he set about refurbishing with extraordinary panache and vision, dressing it up with dragon imagery. The secrets of the equally sublime apartments and roof terrace were finally opened to visitors in 2002.

Round the corner on C. d'Aragó is the Fundació Antoni Tàpies, a modern art gallery. A prototype red-brick Modernista building, its roof is decorated with a mad looping wire sculpture that's particularly remarkable when lit up at night.

Further up the Passeig on the right-hand side is Casa Milà, better known as La Pedrera, a honey-white show-stopping cornerpiece apartment block by Gaudí. Its stonework is sculpted so that its windows look like mini-caves, with contrasting black ironwork (another Gaudí speciality) forming balconies cast like fishing nets. The insides are also a must-see.

AROUND TOWN

Then it's around the corner, turning right onto C. del Rosselló – stopping briefly to take in the gothic palace, Museu de Mùsica – to the maddest house on A. Diagonal: the Casa de les Puntxes, or House of Spikes, a pointy steepled neo-Gothic nightmare. Shiver, then keep walking along Diagonal, turning left down C. de Mallorca. Sanctuary is in the looming form of the Sagrada Família.

Set aside plenty of time to pay homage, to marvel at its size and unworldly beauty, and to queue for the lift to the top of the spires. When you are done, the best vantage point for photographs is from the A. de Gaudí. This also has the best cafés in which to cool your heels before the next bedazzling landmark, handily perched at the top of this avenue: the Hospital de la Santa Creu i Sant Pau, by Domènech i Montaner.

With its monolithic brick pavilions set in sprawling grounds, this is a Modernista head-spinner, a working hospital whose intricate tiled buildings are architectural aromatherapy, calming to the very soul. Designated a World Heritage Site, it's a magnificent mini-city worth an hour of idling time.

If you've got the stamina or the inclination, it's a 20-minute walk downhill from here along C. dels Dos de Maig to Els Encants, an unprepossessing flea market selling all sorts of junk and secondhand treasure. Bear in mind that the best bargains are to be had in the early morning (it opens at 8am), and do your Eixample tour accordingly – in reverse, if scouring's more your thing than sightseeing.

La Pedrera

☕ Out to Lunch

You're never going to go hungry in the Eixample. The Passeig de Gràcia is lined with Basque tapas chains (like **Tapa Tapa, Ba Ba Ree Ba, Qu Qu, Txapela**) and British-style sandwich bars like **Fresh & Ready. Café Torino** (see p.76) is a popular and pricey crowd-watching spot for a coffee and a bite.

Alternatively, the **El Fornet d'en Rossend** chain dotted around the Eixample offers a Med interpretation of a British tea room, with a series of slightly sterile drawing room salons, and newspapers on rollers. Great for a quick restorative *pa amb tomàquet* (baguette rubbed with tomato), cake or muffin.

For a square meal, the best deal is at **Castro** (see pp.69–70) in the Gaixample. The gay-run restaurant, thoughtfully decorated with chains and handcuffs, offers a varied and reasonably priced set lunch menu. The style set also frequent **Tenorio** (see p.75), an international brasserie with a velvet-rope enclave of outdoor tables.

At **Comme Bio** (see p.75) you can get a lunch that will make you feel truly good about yourself. It may not look much and it'll cost you but the tofu and salads are tasty and healthy and light if the weather's killing you.

Around the Sagrada Família, ignore the touristy snack bars in the immediate surrounding area and head instead for **Babilonia** on Av. de Gaudí. You get a perfect view of the cathedral from the terrace tables as you wait for your plate of steaming pasta to arrive.

Time to snack

THE GAIXAMPLE

Barcelona's gay village is relatively compact, occupying a couple of blocks of the left-hand Eixample – and known colloquially as the Gaixample. The streets around C. Consell de Cent and C. Muntaner are peppered with gay bars, restaurants, shops, saunas and the occasional gay *hostal*. However, except for the odd rainbow flag, you'd never know it by walking around by day – these streets are residential and only take on a pink hue after hours.

FOLLOWING GAUDÍ'S EIXAMPLE

If there's one man who can be said to have built Barcelona as many picture it in their mind's eye, it is Antonio Gaudí, the Modernista architect whose creamily spired Sagrada Família cathedral is the city's emblematic landmark. Though the Modernisme style was championed by many Catalan architects, Gaudí's influence is keenest felt in the city, nowhere more starkly than in the Eixample (pronounced Eh-zham-pluh), the 19th-century quarter which contains most of his important private commissions.

OUTLINES

Dramatic detail

CASA AMATLLER / CENTRE DEL MODERNISME

ℹ️ Passeig de Gràcia 41
📞 93 488 01 39
www.bcn.es
🕐 Mon–Sat 10am–7pm; Sun & public holidays 10am–2pm
🚇 Metro: Passeig de Gràcia. Bus: 7, 16, 17, 22, 24, 28 🎟️ Free

Modernista architect Puig i Cadafalch's Gothic contribution to the block of houses known as Mansana de la Discòrdia, commissioned by competing bourgeois families in clashing styles. Inside, there's an information centre selling books of discount coupons to major Modernista landmarks like the Sagrada Família and La Pedrera.

CASA BATLLÓ

ℹ️ Passeig de Gràcia 43
📞 93 488 06 66
www.casabatllo.es
🕐 Daily 9am–8pm
🚇 Metro: Passeig de Gràcia. Bus: 7, 16, 17, 22, 24, 28 🎟️ €16

Gaudí at his most emblematic. Since the dragon-like building was opened up to visitors for the 150th anniversary of his birth, the public can now not only enjoy the shimmering exterior, but also the subterranean, Captain Nemo-esque hallway, fish-scale walls, a succession of increasingly grand wood-panelled drawing rooms in the Modernista style, plus the lavish, multi-coloured reliefs in the courtyard.

FUNDACIÓ ANTONI TÀPIES

ℹ️ C. Aragó 255
📞 93 487 03 15
🕐 Tues–Sun 10am–8pm
🚇 Metro: Passeig de Gràcia. Bus: 7, 16, 17, 22, 24, 28
🎟️ €4.20

A former printworks and an early Modernista work by Domènech i Montaner in bare brick and iron. It now houses a curious collection of contemporary Catalan and non-Western art – as well as the 'greatest hits' of Miró's contemporary, Antoni Tàpies: a table pinned to the wall, a wardrobe of clothes, more clothes but daubed with paint and draped over a chair. You get the idea. If anguished modern art is not your thing, content yourself with the exterior – the roof sculpture, a jungle of iron loops, is particularly stunning at night.

CASA MILÁ/LA PEDRERA

ℹ️ Passeig de Gràcia 92, C. de Provença 261
📞 90 240 09 73
www.funcaixacat.org
🕐 Daily 10am–8pm
🚇 Metro: Diagonal. Bus: 7, 16, 17, 22, 24, 28
🎟️ €8

Marvel at Gaudí's undulating stone exterior, then see his genius at work inside. The courtyards, loft and rooftop (which is tiled using hundreds of broken Cava bottles) are all open to the public, as is one of the apartments (El Pis de la Pedrera), furnished in the Modernista style. Entry to the temporary exhibitions is free, accessible via the fantastic stairwell. In summer (July to September), the roof terrace becomes a vibey bar. Book a table in advance and expect to pay about €10 for the stupendous views.

Fundació Antoni Tàpies

CASA DE LES PUNTXES

ℹ️ A. Diagonal 416–420
✖️ Closed to the public
Ⓜ️ Metro: Verdaguer.
Buses: 20, 39, 45, 47

It's not the mock-medieval castle-like façade that's the pull here (accomplished in pretty brickwork though it is), but the turrets topped off with syringe-like needles from which Puig i Cadafalch's Casa Terrades gets its 'House of Spikes' nickname. Irregular in shape and decidedly untheatrical, de les Puntxes is a stark contrast to the more flamboyant, playful examples of Modernista architecture.

LA SAGRADA FAMÍLIA

See pp.13–14.

HOSPITAL DE SANT PAU

ℹ️ C. Sant Antoni María Claret 167
📞 93 291 90 00
✖️ Open daily
Ⓜ️ Metro: Hospital de Sant Pau. Bus: 15, 19, 20, 35, 45, 47, 50, 51, 92

Not only a prime example of Modern-isme in all its bricked glory, but a working hospital with no two wards the same. The entrance hall is stippled with gorgeous pink ceramics, and you'll need to set aside at least half an hour to wander the solemn gardens, the cobbled streets and subterr-anean accessways.

ELS ENCANTS

ℹ️ Plaça de les Glòries Catalanes
✖️ Mon, Wed, Fri, Sat, 9am–6pm Ⓜ️ Metro: Glòries. Bus 7, 56

A buzzy flea market in one of the Eixample's most unprepossessing corners. Go early to rummage among the stock, or stand back and watch local characters socialising.

Fountain of delight

La Rambla

Barcelona's most famous street is its magnificent mile-long café and tree-lined artery cutting through the heart of the Old City (Ciutat Vella), from Plaça de Catalunya to the sea. But in the 14th century, long before it became a fashionable boulevard on which to promenade (or *ramblejeant* in Catalan), it was a covered sewer. The stink lingered on, especially noticeable during the dark years of Franco's reign. Then it was more a magnet for hookers, touts and pickpockets – and elements of all three remain today.

To the east of La Rambla is the Barri Gòtic, a maze of medieval streets whose sights are worth a day's exploration in their own right. (See pp.37–43.) This chapter, then, will take you for a walk along that city's celebrated address, with diversions into the once-seedy former merchant district of El Raval to its west, now an up-and-coming arty quarter. When strolling the Rambla, the trick is to take your time. There's no need to rush, you're on Barcelona time. The chances are the crowds won't let you move off at your usual walking pace anyway…

A DAY OUT

Most visitors to the Rambla (that is, those not staying in its numerous budget hotels and hostels) pour out of Catalunya metro, the landmark fountain-strewn square linking the old town with the new. Along the Rambla de les Canaletes – the first of five seamlessly connected strips that make up the Rambla – the human traffic is heaviest. Tourists gather at the Font de les Canaletes, a fountain from which all visitors are invited to drink in order to ensure their safe return to the city.

Next is the Rambla dels Estudis, where the general hustle and bustle is given a new soundtrack provided by the twitter of caged birds, hence its nickname La Rambla dels Ocells. If the sight of scrawny parrots and strung-up chickens on sale at the market stalls here is upsetting, nip down C. Bonsuccés – a favourite for second-hand vinyl and world music junkies – into the Raval district. You can easily lose the crowds by slipping into its sleek museum, Museu d'Art Contemporani de Barcelona (MACBA). On this side of the Rambla, there are also many fine newish *plaças* (squares) to discover.

Back on the main drag, where La Rambla dels Estudis becomes La Rambla de Sant Josep (better known as La Rambla de las Flores, thanks to its abundance of flower stalls), is the Església de Betlem, a 17th-century remnant built when the boulevard was lined with churches rather than cafés. Its sorry appearance today belies its recent past; it was looted and burned out during the Civil War. For those with an interest in

La Rambla

contemporary art, the nearby converted Palau de Virreina is an increasingly popular stop-off, thanks to a hip new curator.

If you're missing the roar of the crowds, carry on to the Mercat de Sant Josep, the lively, iron-framed food market known as La Boqueria, which is a feast for all the senses. Go shopping for the freshest fruit and veg, as well as every foodstuff imaginable, from sticky sweets like *turròn* (a brittle, nutty nougat) to whole suckling pigs, which hang from the deco fixtures. The small traders' bars dotted around the edge are good, authentic places to have a counter-top breakfast.

The halfway point of the Rambla is marked by a colourful street mosaic by Joan Miró, but don't forget to look up, too. Here, the experimental Bruno Quadros Building is decorated with Chinese dragons and parasols (now a bank, it used to be an umbrella shop). Over the road is the Escribà patisserie, housed in an exquisite Modernist *casa* with blue mosaic glittering around the door. Pop in and marvel at the cakes on display, or have a restorative coffee out the back. (See p.61.) Then head down C. Hospital and find some peace on the Rambla de Raval, a promenade fit for the 21st century: all smooth white concrete, shady palms, and empty except for skateboarders.

Back on the Rambla proper, by the Liceu metro station, begins the lower half, which is a more restrained affair, with fewer swarming crowds. The landmark on Rambla dels Caputxins, the longest of all the Ramblas, is the Gran Teatre del Liceu opera house, rebuilt in 1999 according to original designs after it was razed by a fire. Ask in the foyer for a tour of the splendid auditorium; unless you've booked in advance, it's unlikely you'll get a seat for that night's performance.

For those who can't wait for the Barri Gòtic tour (see pp.37–43), now's a good time to nip through the nearby arched entrance into Plaça Reial, an arcaded but disappointingly unseemly café-edged square full of tourists, tramps and card sharks, but whose centrepiece is the Font de les Tres Gràcies, Gaudí's first civic commission.

Then head for the Palau Güell, an early Modernista building by Gaudí, tucked along Carrer Nou de la Rambla. It is remarkable not only because it is one of his few major buildings outside the Eixample, but because in its mix of medieval and Moorish styles, Gaudí explored what would become his trademark use of decoration inspired by nature, such as columns of brick shaped like palm trees.

Next along is La Rambla de Santa Mónica, which retains its red-light reputation.

Before we reach the end of the Rambla, get your cameras ready for the wooden Teatre Principal, Barcelona's first theatre, built in the 16th century. Then it's on to the Mirador de Colón (across the busy Passeig de Colom), a 19th-century column topped by a statue of Christopher Columbus, inexplicably pointing not to a new world he discovered, but Italy. From the viewing platform at the top, accessible by a rickety and tiny lift, there are great views across the Mediterranean, especially if you don't have the stomach for those from the Montjuïc cable car. (See p.51.)

Out to Lunch

The Rambla isn't blessed with many exciting lunch options, with most places more interested in convenience than quality. The **Pans & Company** sandwich chain, of which there are a number on the Rambla, offer hot-filled *bocadillos* (baguettes) and good-value meal deals.

But the best lunch option is the psychedelic vegetarian outpost **Juicy Jones**, which offers a tasty and varied three-course *menú del dia*. This is usually a soup of the day, plus a mix of healthy salads, spicy dips and a rice course, finished off with a slice of chocolate cake – all for less than €10.

If you're just after a *tallat* and *crescent* (espresso and croissant) to tide you over, you will be spoilt for choice. Try the standing-only coffee bar, **Viena**, popular with local businesspeople by day. The gay place to be (though you'd not know it until the evening) is **Café de L'Opera**, which has a beautiful roof and painted mirrors covered with Deco figurines. The bar seats are often propped up by quiet newspaper-reading types and loud queens. The shine is rather taken off by the fruit machine.

One of the busiest meeting points in town, inexplicably to some, is **Café Zurich**, at the top of La Rambla, where accordionists stalk the terrace tables populated by Dutch sailors and British football fans. But there's always the self-service **La Rotonda**, on top of El Corte Inglés, notable if only for its ringside views across the city.

Fancy something distinctly Catalan? Have a pastry and *xocolata* (hot chocolate) in the late afternoon at a *granja* milk bar. One of the most celebrated is the **Granja M Viader** in the Raval. Don't worry if your Catalan isn't up to ordering – simply point to something on the drinks menu: it'll be hot, sweet and slip down a treat.

PANS & COMPANY
- Rambla 84 and 123
- 93 317 54 33 / 93 301 66 21 Metro: Liceu

JUICY JONES
- C. Cardenal Casañas 7
- 93 302 43 30
- Daily 10am–midnight
- Metro: Liceu

CAFÉ VIENA
- La Rambla 115
- 93 349 9800
- Metro: Liceu

CAFÉ DE L'OPERA
- La Rambla 74
- 93 302 41 80
- Mon–Fri 8.30am– 2pm; Sat-Sun 8.30am–3pm
- Metro: Liceu
- No credit cards

CAFÉ ZURICH
- Plaça de Catalunya 1
- 93 317 91 53 June–end Oct, Mon–Fri 8am–1am, Sat-Sun 10am–1am; End Oct–May Mon–Fri, 8am–11pm, Sat 8am–midnight Metro: Catalunya

LA ROTONDA
- 9th floor, El Corte Inglés, Plaça de Catalunya. (See pp.59–60.)

GRANJA M VIADER
- C. d'En Xucla 4
- Mon 5pm–8.45pm, Tues–Sat 9am–1.45pm, 5pm–8.45pm Metro: Liceu, Catalunya

OUTLINES

MUSEU D'ART CONTEMPORANI DE BARCELONA (MACBA)

ⓘ Plaça dels Àngels 1
☎ 93 412 08 10
www.macba.es
⊗ Late Sept–late June, Mon, Wed–Fri 11am–7.30pm, Sat 10am–8pm, Sun 10am–3pm; late June–late Sept, Mon, Wed–Fri 11am–8pm, Sat 10am–8pm, Sun 10am–3pm Ⓜ Metro: Catalunya
Ⓥ From €4 to €7.50

Houses a collection of important works from Catalan artists of the latter half of the 20th century. Unlike most of Barcelona's museums, this one opens on Mondays (though not Tuesdays).

PALAU DE LA VIRREINA

ⓘ La Rambla 99
☎ 93 316 10 00
⊗ Tues–Sat 11am–8.30pm, Sun 11am–3pm
Ⓜ Metro: Liceu
Ⓥ Free

This 18th-century palace, the former home of a Peruvian diplomat, now houses an inventive photography, music and graphics museum. Its most impressive display is of the centuries-old giant dolls used in the city's street carnival dating back to 1320.

MERCAT DE SANT JOSEP (LA BOQUERIA)

See p.31.

BRUNO QUADROS BUILDING

ⓘ La Rambla, 82 (corner C. Cardenal Casañas)
Ⓜ Metro: Liceu

The sober façade of this corner mansion house was remodelled into something decidedly more

La Rambla

prankster-like in the late 19th century. The experimental motifs, such as the dragon streetlamp and decorative umbrella poked into the stonework, keep the tourists snap-happy.

GRAN TEATRE DEL LICEU

ℹ️ La Rambla 51–59
📞 93 485 99 00
www.liceubarcelona.com/eng
🕙 Guided tours 10am
🚇 Metro: Liceu
💶 €6

Barcelona's sumptuous 19th-century opera house rose from its ashes in 1999 (not for the first time), after a meticulous reconstruction restored its façade and interior, such is its emblematic symbolic value to the city. On a performance night, the Rambla is snarled up with Catalan ladies in their furs and fineries, and their dicky-bowed husbands. Ask at reception about the occasional guided tours of the auditorium.

PALAU GÜELL

ℹ️ C. Nou de la Rambla 3–5
📞 93 317 39 74
🕙 Guided tours only, Nov–Mar Mon–Sat 10am–4.30pm; Apr–Oct Mon–Sat 10am–6.15pm; Closed Sundays. Tours every 15 minutes last 1 hour
🚇 Metro: Liceu
💶 €3

Built as a residence for Gaudí's rich patron, the mock medieval mansion has plenty of modern design elements to thrill: elegant wood floors, funnel-shaped brickwork in the shape of palm trees, and a magnificent rooftop. There's also a

Large landmark – the Mirador de Colón

tunnel that connects in to the hotel over the road (sadly closed to the public). One of Gaudí's earliest major works, it is a very popular attraction (admission is by guided tour only) and day tickets are strictly rationed; best arrive before 11am to ensure you get in. In any case, it's worth checking out the wrought-iron gates, which are spectacular in their workmanship and almost mystic asymmetricality.

TEATRE PRINCIPAL
ℹ️ La Rambla 27
📞 93 301 47 50
Ⓜ️ Metro: Drassanes

Barcelona's earliest surviving theatre, notable for its curved three-part façade decorated with the busts of famous actors.

MIRADOR DE COLÓN
ℹ️ Plaça Portal de la Pau
📞 93 302 52 24
☀️ Jun–Sept, daily 9am–8.30pm; Oct–May daily 10am–6.30pm
Ⓜ️ Metro: Drassanes €2

The world's largest shrine to Christopher Columbus was built to commemorate the discovery of the Americas. The statue

at its top is made from melted-down cannons taken from the castle on Montjuïc. Though it's often shrouded by scaffolding, most visitors are content to cram into the four-man lift, which whizzes to the viewing platform, for fantastic bird's-eye panoramas across the sea and the city.

Don't mistake this crapper for a souvenir

The Catalan Crapper

It's the ultimate tacky Barcelona souvenir: a clay figurine of a cute little fella answering the call of nature, squatting with his trousers round his ankles. Say hello to the Catalan Crapper. Souvenir shops along La Rambla and around the La Seu cathedral (see p.15) delight tourists with *El Caganer*, who's usually dressed in a floppy felt hat and sucking on a Sherlock Holmes pipe, but is variously dolled up as priest, nun or fireman, or even kitted out in the red and blue strip of FC Barça. At Christmas, even church nativities in Barcelona include a crapper in the congregation worshipping the virgin birth. Don't ask why, it's a Catalan thing… and you know someone back home who'll want one.

High rise life in the old city

The Old City

Until the end of the 19th century, the Ciutat Vella, or Old City, was the heart of Barcelona, its citizens penned in by stone walls built by the Romans, who founded 'Barcino' 2,000 years ago. The maze of streets that sprang up within this confine over the centuries kept to the tight map left by the settlers, so today, the Old City is one of the best preserved medieval centres in Europe. It serves both as a reminder of Barcelona's Roman heritage and offers a window to its 'golden years' between the 12th and 15th centuries, when it became a thriving trading post and home to Catalonia's all-powerful courtly kings.

The Old City is roughly hewn into a series of neighbourhoods, each with their own distinct flavour and antiquities, with the 13th-century La Seu cathedral at its Gothic heart. Most appealing are the Barri Gòtic, the largely freeze-framed medieval hub where sections of that Roman wall, eventually torn down in the 19th century, can still be seen; La Ribera, or waterfront, that was home to Barcelona's merchant city; and El Born, the tiny cobbled quarter that has been 'reborn' in recent years after an influx of unusual boutiques and galleries. The Old City is more than a maze of scrubbed-up medieval alleyways. It's always throbbing with life, by day packed out with trendy shoppers spilling out from the stylish boutiques along C. Avinyó, then a noisy magnet for barflies on the starting blocks for an all-night party.

This walk will take in the Old City neighbourhoods enclosed by La Rambla to the left and Via Laietana to the right. For El Raval, the largest and westernmost Old City neighbourhood, see Around Town: La Rambla (p.29).

A DAY OUT

You don't so much need a map as a time machine to keep track of where you are in the Old City. Here, every street shows its age and the part it played in the evolution of BC Barcino into style capital BCN. One of the city's greatest pleasures is getting caught up in the Barri Gòtic's tight web of narrow alleyways. You are advised, then, to improvise your own route based on this walk.

Let's start at the top of the Old City and work around anticlockwise. Hop off the metro at Catalunya and head along the wide high-street shopping avenue Portal de l'Àngel, looking out for C. Montsió, a small side street that's home to one of the most historic cafés, Els Quatre Gats (The Four Cats). Once you've had your first coffee of the day, it's over Via

Laietana and into La Ribera for a quick tour of the Palau de la Música Catalunya, a highly decorated Modernista music hall.

Dazzled by the Palau, set off down Via Laietana, and hang a right along C. Dr Joaquim Pou. This brings you to the Catedral de Barcelona, also regarded by some as the city's finest cathedral not by Gaudí, which was built in the 13th century (though it has a

Gothic lamppost

Modernista stained-glass window by a Gaudí contemporary).

Now a cobbled junction, this is the high watermark of internecine Catalan politics. Here you'll find the Palau de la Generalitat, home of the regional government, and the Ajuntament, or City Hall, directly opposite.

A few doors away on C. Ferran, at number 42, is a plaque marking the birthplace of Catalonia's most revered artist of the 20th century, Joan Miró. For another such landmark, keep heading towards La Rambla to Plaça Reial, a café-lined square whose ornate wrought-iron lampposts were designed by the young Antonio Gaudí. If art's not your thing, nip along C. Avinyó instead for a spot of credit-card crunching in the designer boutiques.

At the foot of C. Avinyó is the towering Església de la Mercè, topped off by a statue of the Virgin that appears to float. It's worth comparing with the Església de Santa Maria del Mar, the best preserved church in gloomy Catalan Gothic style, a five-minute walk away in La Ribera on the other side of Via Laietana. Mind the traffic that hares along it.

Because of its proximity to the port, La Ribera was once the working hub of the city, and its mercantile history is now reflected in its street names, which reference tanners, wool combers, grain traders and even semolina-makers. Today, it's home to a cluster of great museums, including the self-explanatory Museu Picasso and the Museu Tèxtil i d'Indumentària, which explores Catalan fashion through the ages, as well as the importance of its textile industry.

Keep heading along C. Montcada to check out the newly restored Mercat Santa Caterina, Barcelona's oldest market, then double back on yourself to spend the rest of the afternoon shopping in El Born.

Prized in fashion magazines the world over for its street style, the cobbled and Gothic-pillared Passatge del Born and its side streets buzz with chat, the clacking of heels and the pop-pop of scooters. Don't miss the inspiring curving lamppost-like memorial sculpture, topped with flame, in Plaça del Fosser de les Morreres, dedicated to those who died defending Barcelona during the 18th-century Spanish siege; or Plaça del Duc de Medicaneli, where Pedro Almodóvar shot his Oscar-winning *Todo Sobre Mi Madre* (*All About My Mother*).

Out to Lunch

Lunch is served

You're on holiday so there's nothing wrong with a little sparkling white wine (it's not really *xampan*) for lunch, served up with a few little plates of tapas, at **El Xampanyet**. Depending on the hour this place can be a real scrum but tourists are light on the ground and the surroundings are picturesque if you like a barrel and some weird bric-a-brac.

The most filling brunch in town can be had at slightly boho **Bagel Shop**. Alternatively, there are plenty of bleeding-edge cafés in El Born. Try **Sandwiches + Friends**, a relaxed restaurant-café with a popular outdoor terrace that's great for spotting style-setters.

For a full meal, try **Vildsvin**, a modern *taverna* serving up taste-clashes from all over Europe. Pick and mix your own lunch menu: will it be Viking fish soup followed by Bologna sausages and a Bavarian pastry ring, or Flemish broth followed by Galician hamburgers? If you can't decide, there is a *menú del dia* (prix fixe) with a beer. The best vegetarian deals can be had at the Museu Tèxtil's cool brick courtyard café.

EL XAMPANYET
C. Montcada 22
93 319 70 03
Metro: Jaume 1

THE BAGEL SHOP
C. Canuda 25
93 302 41 61
Metro: Catalunya

SANDWICHES + FRIENDS
Passeig del Born 27
93 310 07 86
Metro: Jaume I

VILDSVIN L'ANTIGA TAVERNA
C. Ferran 38
93 317 94 07
Metro: Liceu

TÈXTIL CAFÉ
Museu Tèxtil, C. Montcada 12
93 268 25 98
Closed Mondays
Metro: Jaume I

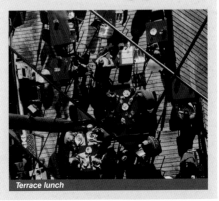
Terrace lunch

AROUND TOWN

OUTLINES

ELS QUATRE GATS

- **ⓘ** C. Montsió 3
- **☎** 93 302 41 40
- **🕐** Mon–Sat 8am–2am
- **Ⓜ** Metro: Catalunya

This is where the local bohemian intelligentsia – including Picasso, who designed the menu front – came to sup and exchange revolutionary ideas in *fin-de-siècle* Barcelona. A landmark in its own right, it is notable for being Puig i Cadafalch's first Modernista building.

PALAU DE LA MÚSICA CATALUNYA

- **ⓘ** C. Sant Francesc de Paula 2 **☎** 93 295 72 00
- www.palaumusica.org
- **🕐** Guided tours: 10am–3.30pm daily **Ⓜ** Metro: Urquinaona **🎟** €8
- See p.92.

CATEDRAL DE BARCELONA (LA SEU)

See p.15.

MUSEU D'HISTÒRIA DE LA CIUTAT

- **ⓘ** Plaça del Rei
- **☎** 93 315 11 11
- www.bcn.es/cultura
- **🕐** Oct–May Tues–Sat 10am–2pm, 4pm–8pm, Sun and hols 10am–2pm; June–Sept Tues–Sat 10am–8pm, Sun and hols 10am–2pm

- **Ⓜ** Metro: Jaume I

For an idea of what Roman Barcino would have been like for its inhabitants, take the glass lift beneath the streets for a lively 'virtual' tour of the Roman remains under Plaça del Rei. Includes a reconstruction of how Barcelona looked at the height of its standing in the 15th century.

PALAU DE LA GENERALITAT

- **ⓘ** Plaça de Sant Jaume
- **☎** 93 402 46 17
- www.gencat.net
- **🕐** Guided tours 2nd and 4th Sun, 10.30am–1.30pm
- **Ⓜ** Metro: Jaume 1 **🎟** Free

Home of Catalonia's parliament and its president, who has quarters in this sumptuous 15th-century palace, which also incorporates lively elements of Catalan Gothic. Access is by guided tour only, but worth the queues just to walk around the orange garden.

AJUNTAMENT DE BARCELONA

- **ⓘ** Plaça de Sant Jaume
- **☎** 93 402 70 00
- www.bcn.es **🕐** Sun 10am–2pm **Ⓜ** Metro: Jaume I **🎟** Free

Barcelona's City Hall

was built in the 15th century, at the height of its golden years, though the neo-classical façade was added when the square was opened to the public in the 19th century. Tours take you round the corridors of council power – but it's a surprisingly diverting trawl of architectural styles and flamboyant furnishings. Livelier still is the square in front, which hosts *sardana* dancing displays on Sundays.

ESGLÉSIA DE LA MERCÈ

- **ⓘ** A. de Sarajevo 6–8
- **☎** 93 370 14 13
- **Ⓜ** Metro: Dressanes

Set back from La Ribera's waterfront and a towering presence casting shadows over the Plaça de la Mercè, this Baroque church contains a Gothic statue of Our Lady of Mercy, the Virgin after whom it is named, and a font dedicated to Neptune, showing its links with all things naval. The *plaça* also hosts the ebullient Festival de la Mercè every September.

ESGLÉSIA DE SANTA MARIA DEL MAR

- **ⓘ** Plaça de Santa Maria
- **☎** 93 310 23 90. Concert information 93 319 05 16

⏰ Mon–Sat 9am–1:30pm, 4:30pm–8pm; Sun 9am–2pm, 5pm–8:30pm
🚇 Metro: Jaume I
🎟 Free

With its looming octagonal towers, this grey stone 14th-century church pushed Gothic archictecture to its limit – the supporting columns span widths greater than any other medieval building in the world. Gutted by a fire in the 1800s, its slightly glum air only adds to the hair-shirted majesty. Look out for concerts held here.

MUSEU PICASSO
ℹ C. Montcada 15–23

☎ 93 319 63 10
www.museupicasso.bcn.es
🚇 Metro: Jaume I, Liceu, Arc de Triomf
⏰ Tues–Sat 10am–8pm; Sun 10am–3pm 🎟 €5, free first Sunday of the month

Contains important works from his early life as a painter, but is far sketchier on his Cubism. Blink and you'll miss the Blue and Pink Periods entirely. Good selection of ceramics and engravings, though.

MUSEU TÈXTIL I D'INDUMENTÀRIA
ℹ C. Montcada 12–14
☎ 93 319 76 03

www.museutextil.bcn.es
⏰ Tues–Sat 10am–6pm; Sun and hols 10am–3pm
🚇 Metro: Jaume I
🎟 €3.50, free first Sunday of the month

The city's modern textile and costume museum is a sprightly affair, with a collection of international fabrics, embroideries, lace and tapestries – and an outrageously camp display of men's footwear. Also plays up the impact of Barcelona's textile industry on the world catwalk.

PARC DE LA CIUTADELLA
See p.17.

Picasso mural

Terrific Torre (de Telefónica)

Montjuïc

Montjuïc, the monolithic rock that sprawls to the south of the city, is where Barcelona comes to stretch its legs. An oasis of lush parklands with unbeatable panoramas, it is a perfect place for a stroll or a lazy siesta – there's even a network of open-air escalators to help you up and down its steeper flanks.

Rising up from the Mediterranean and unfeasibly close to the city centre, it was here that much of the 1992 Olympic Games were played out.

Montjuïc holds a strong gay fascination – composer Benjamin Britten wrote a dance suite dedicated to it – thanks mostly to its reputation as the city's busiest cruising ground. Not for nothing do the people of Barcelona refer to it as 'Pink Mountain' – its bushes are alive at all times of the day, and the police don't seem to mind.

A DAY OUT

Let's make this easy by starting at the top and working down. But how do you get to the top of Montjuïc? One of the easiest and quaintest ways is the funicular from Paral-lel metro station to A. Miramar, the main road which snakes around the mountain. (See p.51.) If you think the views across the city from outside Parc de Montjuïc station are awesome, wait until you pick up the nearby cable car that swings passengers up a stage higher, to the Castell de Montjuïc at the summit.

The first optional stop-off comes at the Fundació Joan Miró, an impressive white cliff-edge gallery on A. Miramar built to honour the great Catalan symbolist's reputation, with the express intention of housing a large permanent collection of his most important works. It's a must for Miró fans – but there's also a fantastic roof terrace littered with colourful sculptures that are more fun than chin-strokingly 'deep'.

Further along is the Anella Olímpic, the string of sporting complexes renovated for use during the 1992 Olympic Games: namely the Estadi Olímpic, now the home ground of Barcelona's second soccer team, Espanya, and Piscines Bernat Picornell, the awesome laned indoor and outdoor pools that open to the public for lane swimming (don't forget to pack your kit!). The Plaça d'Europa is dominated by architect Santiago Calatrava's dove-white Torre de Telefònica, a futuristic looping telecom tower, with a *trencadís* mosaic at its base, in deference to Gaudí.

The nearby Palau Nacional houses the Museu Nacional d'Art de Catalunya and a tour lays out the nation's stylistic progression from

Gran Via de les Corts Catalanes

C. de Gava

C. de Sant Moianès

Crta. de la Bordeta

C. de St. Fructós

C. d'Amposta

C. de Mexic

PARC DEL FONT FLORIDA

C. de la

Avinguda del Marqués

Caixa Forum

L'Albi

Museu de les Arts Grafique

Museu de Industrials

Av. de **Font Màgica**

Pavelló Mies van de Rohe

Poble Espanyol

C. de Polvorí

Avinguda

Institut i Jardi Botànic ●

Passeig de les Casca

C. del Ferrocarrils Catalans

C. del Segura

Pl. d'Europa

Piscines Bernat Picornell

de

MNAC 🍴

Museu National d'Art de Catalunya ●

Museu Etnològic

C. de Pedera de Mossol

C. del Foc

C. dels Jocs del 92

PALAU DE SANT JORDI

Pg. Olímpic

Estadi

Estadi

AREA MONTJUÏC

Pg. Olímpic

Galería Olimpica ●

Olimpic

ESTADI DE MO

C. del Doctor Font i roger

Pg. de

Milicia

CEMENTIRI DEL SUD-OEST

PARC DEL MIGDIA

Cas
M

Muse

C. de la Mare de Déu de Port

V. de Circulació Nord

Ronda del Litoral

Monjuïc

Monjuïc

9th-century murals discovered in local monasteries, through the birth of Catalan Gothic as an architectural style, and beyond.

Leave the museum and head left, following the signs for the Poble Espanyol, a 1929 educational theme park showcasing each region of Spain with an artisanal 'village' designed in typical local style; it's quite the tourist trap. Alternatively, to the right is the city's busiest cruising area. In the bushes around the Miró-esque glass sculpture, called Arc de Triomf, is where gay men come to lose their invisible dogs in the undergrowth.

Once you've toured either or both fun parks, double back to the front of the Palau Nacional, take a flight of steps down, and you're at the Font Màgica, a monument to kitsch that hosts a popular son-et-lumière show.

Before we reach the bottom, there's more art to be had, not least in the boxy shape of the Pavelló Barcelona, German architect Ludwig Mies van der Rohe's landmark summer pavilion on A. Marqués de Comillas. Over the road, there's the CaixaForum, a newcomer to the Barcelona art scene, hosting important contemporary exhibitions housed in a crenellated Modernista brick building.

Now we're at the foot of Montjuïc. Walk along the gated boulevard A. Reina Maria Cristina, Plaça d'Espanya. The enormous bullring that dominates the far-right exit of the busy roundabout is currently being transformed into a futuristic leisure centre by British architect Richard Rogers. Tournaments are currently held here only occasionally – bullfighting is seen here as a Spanish rather than a Catalan thing – but there's a small museum for those interested in the history of the 'sport'.

 Out to Lunch

MNAC restaurant receives unusually good reviews for its relaxed lunch service in a stylish, contemporary restaurant.

Work up an appetite for **L'Albí**, which is inside the Poble Espanyol and does a great €12 *menù del dia* of Med fare, or a series of taster plates (*tastet de la casa*) for €15 to introduce you to the Catalan kitchen: *pa amb tomàquet* (oil-drizzled crusty bread rubbed with tomato, a very typical starter), sausage with beans, vermicelli with shellfish, and so on.

For a nice alfresco lunch of nibbles and beers try **La Caseta del Migdia**. Follow the Camí del Mar around Montjuïc until you come across this cute little space with music and hammocks and a very laid-back vibe.

CAFÉ FUNDACIÓ JOAN MIRÓ
A, de l'Estadi 93 329 07 68 Oct–Jun

Tues–Sat 10am–7pm, Sun 10am–2.30pm; Jul–Sept Tues–Sat 10am–8pm, Sun 10am–2.30pm
Espanya

MNAC
(See p.49.)

L'ALBÍ
Inside Poble Espanyol
93 424 93 24
Sat–Thur 12–5pm & 8pm–midnight, closed Fri
Espanya

LA CASETA DEL MIGDIA
Mirador de Migdia, Passeig del Migdia
617 956 572
Bus 55

OUTLINES

MUSEU MILITAR

ⓘ Castell de Montjuïc

☎ 93 329 86 13

☼ Nov–mid-Mar Tues–
Sun 9.30am–5.30pm;
mid-Mar–Oct Tues–Sun
9.30am–8pm Ⓜ Metro:
Paral-lel, then funicular
and teleferic Ⓥ €2.50

Perched at the very
top of Montjuïc, the
former fortress was
used as a detention
and torture centre for
dissenters in the 18th
century after the fall
of Barcelona. It now
houses the last statue
of Franco in the city
(kept out of spitting
distance from have-a-
go members of the
public). If cabinets of
handguns and rifles
aren't your thing,
check out the peerless
city views – and enjoy
the precarious cable
car ride up here. (See
p.51.)

FUNDACIÓ JOAN
MIRÓ

See p.16.

ESTADI OLÍMPIC

ⓘ A de l'Estadi

☎ www.fundaciobarcelona
olimpica.es Ⓜ Metro:
Espanya, then escalators
Ⓥ €2.40. Call ServiCaixa
for match tickets. (See p.91.)

The Olympic stadium
is now the home of
Espanya football club,

whose home matches
are far easier to get
tickets for than the
city's favourite, FC
Barça. Includes a
gallery of Olympic
Games-related
memorabilia.

PISCINES BERNAT
PICORNELL

See p.97.

MUSEU NACIONAL
D'ART DE
CATALUNYA
(MNAC)

ⓘ Palau Nacional

☎ 93 622 03 60

www.mnac.es

☼ Tues–Sat 10am–7pm,
Sun 10am–2.30pm

Ⓜ Metro: Espanya, then
escalators

Ⓥ €4.80

A brief history of
Catalan art, architect-
ure and liturgical
artefacts, presented in
rough chronological

order across 21
galleries in a
magnificent mock-
Baroque palace.
Highlights include the
Romanesque murals
rescued from
Pyrenean churches,
and a Gothic collect-
ion of religious works
commissioned at the
height of Catalonia's
medieval glory.

POBLE ESPANYOL

ⓘ A. Marqués de
Comillas

☎ 93 325 78 66

www.poble-espanyol.com

☼ Mon 9am–8pm,
Tues–Thur 9am–2am,
Fri–Sat 9am–4am, Sun
9am– midnight

Ⓜ Metro: Espanya Ⓥ €7

Curious that you
don't have to leave
Barcelona – which
hates being called
Spanish – for a
whistlestop tour of

Olympic Stadium

Spain. This theme park rejoices in Spanish ways of life, with each area represented by a 'miniature village'. There's a bell tower from Zaragoza, a traditional house from Aragon, and so on. Plazas are peppered with lime trees, the smell of garlic wafts out from the rustic restaurants and feral cats roam about to

MIRÓ'S BLACK MARK

When you're fathoming a colourful canvas by Joan Miró in his Fundació on Montjuïc, think on this: what's behind the meaning of the black asterisk that's a motif in practically every painting he ever did? Nationalists say it's a patriotic stamp representing his allegiance to the 'star of Catalonia'. Nice try – the Catalan star is red. In fact, it's a cheeky signature representing the anus. As a breed, Catalans admit to a slight anal fixation (see p.35), and, for Miró, it just shows that even a serious symbolist likes to have his fun…

add Spanishness. As a concept, it's done with a certain élan that should appeal beyond the usual heritage set. But there is a nagging sense that you're paying to walk around a marketplace. Each village has a visitors' workshop selling local handicrafts, such as printed textiles, hand-blown glass or woven baskets. There are smart restaurants, various good-quality terrace cafés, a juice bar and popcorn stands for snacking. And in the summer, the Poble Espanyol stays open late for drinks and, disconcertingly, holds a legendary gay club night on its main terrace. (See p.88.)

Poble Espanyol

FONT MÁGICA

ℹ️ Plaça d'Espanya
📞 93 291 40 42
www.bcn.es/fonts
🕐 Shows every 30 minutes: May–Sept Thur–Sun 9.30pm– 11.30pm; Mar, April, Oct–early Jan Fri–Sat 7pm–9pm

Ⓜ️ Metro: Espanya
Ⓥ Free

A mere fountain (albeit a slightly grandiose example) during the week; on weekend evenings (Thur–Sun in summer) it is spectacularly lit up as the Font's water jets are made to dance and spray to the strains of cheesy pop tracks and classical overtures. Come early to elbow your way to the best vantage point, and prepare to coo and cuddle up to a loved one.

PAVELLÓ BARCELONA

See p.18.

CAIXAFORUM

ℹ️ A. Marqués de Comillas 6–8
📞 93 476 86 00
www.fundacio.lacaixa.es
🕐 Tues–Sun 10am–8pm
Ⓜ️ Metro: Espanya
Ⓥ Free

A new gallery inside a renovated Modernista textile mill that houses a collection of European contemporary art, including an installation by Joseph Beuys. Blockbuster retrospectives of internationally renowned artists find their crowds right here.

Joyriding

Part of the fun of Montjuïc is getting there. The number 50 bus is a popular choice – a little too popular in summer, as it's often full by the time it picks up at Plaça d'Espanya. The Bus Turistic and the Tren Montjuïc – not a train but a truck-drawn trolley bus – also wend the same route along the A.

Trip to the top

Marqués de Comillas. Both beat flagging cabs at the busy Espanya roundabout. Or you could always walk, leaving the outdoor escalators to take the strain.

More fun is the Funicular de Montjuïc, which leaves from Paral·lel metro, travelling up its own near-vertical tunnel to its own station on A. Miramar. You won't get great views from your seat, but it grinds up the hill in no time. Thrillseekers should then try the teleferic up to the hilltop castle.

And then there's the antique cable car. The Transbordador Aeri whisks tourists, sardine-like in its creaky carriages, from stations in Barceloneta and Port Vell, to the cliff edge near Plaça l'Armada. It's so old – and nail-biting – that it is shut down with the first gust of wind.

TREN MONTJUÏC

From Plaça d'Espanya to Miramar

93 415 60 20

Mid April–mid Sept 11am–10pm daily. Every 30 mins

€1.80 single

FUNICULAR DE MONTJUÏC

From Paral·lel metro to A. Miramar

93 443 08 59

www.tmd.net

June–Oct daily 11am–10pm; Nov–April Sat–Sun 10.45am–8pm;

May daily 10.45am–8pm

€1.70 single, €2.50 return

TELEFÈRIC DE MONTJUÏC

From Estació Funicular on Av. Miramar to Castell

93 443 08 59

www.tmb.net

June–mid Sept daily 11.15am–9pm; mid Sept–Oct, April, May daily 11am–7.15pm; Nov–Mar Sat–Sun 11am–7.15pm

€3.20 single, €4.50 return

TRANSBORDADOR AERI

From Torre de Jaume I (Port Vell) and Torre Sant Sebastià (Barceloneta) to Miramar (and vice versa)

93 441 48 20

Mid June–mid Sept daily 10.45am–7.15pm; mid Sept–mid Oct, Mar–mid June daily 10.30am–5.45pm; mid Oct–Feb daily 10.30am–5.30pm. Every 15 mins

€7.50 single, €9 return

Windsurfer sets out

The Seaside

Barcelona's long strip of Mediterranean seaside takes in four neighbourhoods. Port Vell, or Old Port, was once a grim cargo dockland before it was demolished for the Olympic Games and replaced by graceful boulevards lined with restaurants and street sculptures. Barceloneta is the triangular neighbourhood traditionally home to fishermen, before the yuppies started muscling in; there's a swish marina, but cut through the tight-gridded streets to hit the beach and there's a residual working-class flavour. The Vila Olímpica, seafront home to the athletes at the 1992 Games, is now populated by the city's strolling classes, who come for the wide seafront walkways, as well as the shops, restaurants, bars and clubs around the Port Olímpic (there are more nightspots here than in any other part of the city, albeit fairly colour-by-numbers affairs).

The fourth neighbourhood, furthest from the city centre, is Poble Nou (or New Village), a working-class district on the up and up. For now, its greatest asset is its seafront, with beaches seething with sun-seekers in summer, including a nudist section colonised mostly by gays, Platja de Mar Bella, tucked behind the Base Náutica.

As the seafront stretches for four kilometres, consider hopping on a bus. The 41 from Plaça Catalunya will take you to Mar Bella and beyond, while the 36 from the Mirador de Colón gives a comprehensive street-level tour of Port Vell.

A DAY OUT

First things first: make sure you've packed a beach towel and are wearing comfy sandals and plenty of sunscreen. This walk is 10 kilometres as a round trip – so you're guaranteed to catch the sun. Start at the foot of the Ramblas (nearest metro station is Drassanes). Before you hit the beach, it's worth getting your bearings with a trip up the Mirador de Colón, the monument marking the spot where Columbus is said to have landed in 1492 on his return from America – though he's pointing the wrong way (see p.35). If you're lucky, you'll be able to pinpoint a free stretch of beach...

Then you've got a choice. You could walk towards *Cap de Barcelona* (*Barcelona Head*), the landmark Pop Art sculpture by Roy Lichtenstein, along Moll de la Fusta, the palm-fronded waterfront that roars with traffic. Far nicer is to stroll out onto the Rambla del Mar, an 'extension' of the Rambla proper made of wooden drawbridges which swing around to let ships into Port Vell. On a sunny day the wavy walkways – very moderno – buzz with pedestrians heading for the Moll d'Espanya wharf. This complex showcases attractions like the Maremàgnum shopping centre, an IMAX cinema and

N

RAMBLA DE MAR

Moll d'Espanya

Pg. Colom

Pg. Isabel II

C. Balboa

Av. Marquès de l'Argentera

Pg. Circumval·lació

PARC DE LA CIUTADELLA

PARC ZOOLÒGIC

Romon Trus Fargas

Marina

Joan Miró

Av. Icària

Av. Bogatell

Frederic Mompou

Pl. Tirant Lo Blanc

Jaume Vicens i Vives

Dr. Trueta

Taulat

Carmen Amaya

Salvador Espriu

PARC DEL POBLENOU

Pg. Calvell

Pg. Garcia i Faria

Ronda Litoral

Taulat

Pg. Marítim del la Mar Bella

PARC ESPORTIU MAR BELL

PLATJA NOVA MAR BELLA

PLATJA MAR BELLA

PLATJA DEL BOGATELL

Pg. Marítim del Bogatell

PLATJA NOVA ICÀRIA

Pg. Marítim Nova Icària

PORT OLÍMPIC

PLATJA DE LA BARCELONETA

Ronda Litoral

PARC DE LA BARCELONETA

Pg. Marítim Barceloneta

C. Almirall Cervera

Pg. Joan de Borbó

Pl. del Mar

PLATJA SANT SEBASTIÀ

PLATJA SANT MIQUEL

Europe's largest aquarium. It is also a popular night-time hangout for clubbers who flock here to its myriad bars and discos.

Once you've been wowed by Moll d'Espanya's shininess and spanking newness, it's time for a gear change. Follow the Moll Dispòsit, past the Palau del Mar which houses the Museu d'Història de Catalunya, around to Barceloneta. The fishing neighbourhood of 'Little Barcelona' is so called because it was created from land reclaimed from the sea in the 18th century. Today, it also houses the pretty Port Vell Marina, whose mooring bays are lined with super-expensive yachts and whose main drag, Passeig Joan de Borbó, is a good place to catch some rays while eating the freshest fish dishes in town (albeit expensively).

At the far tip of Passeig Joan de Borbó, the beaches begin. The Torre de Sant Sebastià on Platja Sant Sebastià is where you can catch the Trasbordador Aeri cable car up to (or down from) Montjuïc. The viewing platform at the top of the station offers great views along the shoreline. At some indiscernible point, Platja Sant Sebastià becomes Platja Barceloneta, which attracts a disproportionate number of same-sex couples amid a sea of oiled-up bodies. The serious posing goes on along the strip near Plaça del Mar.

If you're on a go-slow when walking the length of Platja Barceloneta, admiring the sun-splashed physiques as well as eye-catching beach sculptures as you go, it'll be a good 25 minutes before you reach the Port Olímpic. Alternatively, you can do it double-quick on rollerblades (to hire, visit Al Punt de Trobada in Poble Nou). Aside from the azure-blue sea, sights worth drinking in include Hotel Arts, Spain's tallest building, and its neighbouring 'twin' towerblock; Frank Gehry's fish monument; the street markets, selling cheap ties, knock-off CDs and surprisingly good Louis Vuitton rip-offs; and the shops in the Marina Village stocking essential beach gear. El Centre de la Vila Port Olímpic also has one of the best cinemas for English-language blockbusters, the Yelmo Cineplex – which makes it worth coming back for an evening out. (See p.92.)

Once past the port, there's a clear run of well-kept beaches, tree-lined walkways and intermittent bars and restaurants for a couple of kilometres. The beaches are all blue-flag approved for cleanliness, and very well-appointed with showers, deckchairs, beach volleyball courts, lifeguards (in season) and good disabled access. The crowds thin out the further you venture past Platja Nova Icària and Platja del Bogatell. You'll know you're near the gay nudist beach, Platja Mar Bella, when you hit Base Náutica Mar Bella, Barcelona's centre for water sports. Head past the groups doing up wetsuits and around the shady hillock that provides some privacy for the only spot in town where you can sunbathe nude.

Frank's fish

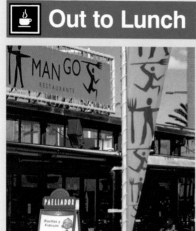

☕ Out to Lunch

Mango munchies

MANGO
ⓘ Platja Nova Icària
☎ 93 221 35 58
Ⓜ Metro: Ciutadella-Vila
Olímpica. Bus 36, 41 🍴 🍸

**XIRINGUITÓ
ESCRIBÀ**
ⓘ Litoral Mar, 42 (Platja
Bogatell) ☎ 93 221 07 29
🕐 Tues–Sat 1pm–
4.30pm & 9pm–11.30pm;
Sun 1pm–4.30pm
Ⓜ Metro: Ciutadella-Vila
Olímpica. Bus 36 🍴 🍸

AGUA
ⓘ Passeig Marítim de la
Barceloneta 30 ☎ 93 225 12
72 🕐 Mon–Thur 1.30pm–
4pm, 8.30pm–midnight;
Fri–Sat 1.30pm–4pm,
8.30pm–1am; Sun
1.30pm–4pm, 8.30pm–
midnight Ⓜ Metro
Barceloneta. Bus 45, 57, 59,
157 🍴 🍸–🍸

Barceloneta is famed for its fish restaurants, especially those facing the marina along Passeig Joan de Borbó, a blissful sun-kissed drag that's perfect for a mid-afternoon stroll to peruse the menus. If you're just after drink and snacks (which means sandwiches, cakes and *cortados*) and can't afford to lose that prime spot on the sand, there are three modern beach bars pitched strategically every few hundred metres along Platja Nova Icària, as well as a couple of popular restaurants set back on the promenade. For *fideuà* (Catalan paella), try **Mango**, a popular (if a little soulless) hang-out with hassled staff and outside

seating that's manna to bothersome street performers. Near Platja Bogatell is **Xiringuitó Escribà**, a spin-off seafood restaurant from the city's famed Escribà patisserie dynasty. (See p.61.) There's a lunchtime tapas menu, and round-the-clock divine desserts, as you'd expect. For fine but informal Catalan dining, ring ahead for a table at Barceloneta's trendiest spot, **Agua**. It has a reasonably priced and popular lunch menu – try the *arròs salvatge amb verdures i gingebre* (wild rice with greens and ginger) – but the deal-clincher is its cool setting right on the beach.

OUTLINES

L'AQUÀRIUM

ℹ️ Moll d'Espanya
☎️ 93 221 74 74
www.aquariumbcn.com
🕐 Mon–Fri 9.30am–9pm,
Sat–Sun (and holidays)
9.30am–9.30pm (June,
Sept), 9.30am–11pm
July–Aug 🚇 Metro:
Drassanes, Barceloneta
💶 €15

The largest aquarium in Europe, where visitors journey to the bottom of the Mediterranean via a series of glass walkways. Sharks sporadically flash their jaws at excitable visitors.

MUSEU D'HISTÒRIA DE CATALUNYA

ℹ️ Palau del Mar, Plaça Pau Vila 3 ☎️ 93 225 47 00
www.en.mhcat.net
🕐 Tues, Thur, Fri, Sat 10am–7pm, Wed 10am–8pm, Sun & public holidays 10am–2.30pm, closed Mon
🚇 Metro: Barceloneta
💶 €3.01

The marina-edged attraction rolls out a visitor-friendly, brief history of Catalonia in a series of engaging and often witty, un-gallery-like rooms: the birth and evolution of the Catalan nation and people from their Roman roots to post-Franco renaissance is explained in highly visual terms.

BASE NÁUTICA DE MAR BELLA

ℹ️ A. Litoral (on Platje Mar Bella) ☎️ 93 221 04 32
www.basenautica.org
🕐 Daily May–Sept, 10am–8pm; Oct–April 10am–4.30pm 🚇 Metro: Poblenou 💶 Individual prices per activity

Windsurfing, kayaking, snorkelling, diving, catamaran sailing… Barcelona's got it all – and the Base Náutica is the one-stop shop for active waterbabies. A 20-minute walk from the old port, where Platja Bogatell meets Platja Mar Bella (look out for the rugged types in wetsuits), come here to rent canoes, surf boards and sailing boats by the hour, or for a week's worth of tuition to brush up on your favourite water sport.

LAS GOLONDRINAS

ℹ️ Portal de la Pau
☎️ 93 442 31 06
www.lasgolondrinas.com
🚇 Metro: Drassanes
💶 Tours from €9.70 per person

Tour operator offering boat trips around the port and along the coast. Departures are every 60 minutes throughout the day, from 11.30am to 6.30pm. Booking is essential. Boats are also available for hire.

THE ORSOM CATAMARAN

☎️ 93 221 82 83
www.barcelona-orsom.com, orsom@barcelona-orsom.com 🚇 Metro: Drassanes 💶 Prices on request

Large 90-person catamaran – the largest in Barcelona – offering daily 90-minute luxury tours of the port and coastline and Sunday-night jazz and banquet cruises.

TRANSBORDADOR AERI CABLE CAR

from Torre de Sant Sebastià See p.51.

HOTEL ARTS

for Frank Gehry's Peix (Fish) monument See p.55.

MIRADOR DE COLÓN

See p.55.

IMAX CINEMA

See p.92.

YELMO CINEMA

See p.92.

The Aquarium

Barcelona: shopping central

All Shopped Out

Once it was Paris, then New York, and more recently London. Now it seems Barcelona is where Europe comes to shop for the latest fashions. According to reports, 43 per cent of visitors' holiday money is spent in the shops – and there are plenty of places to spend.

From the largest department stores and international fashion brand flagships to the smallest independents dotted along Passeig del Born and Plaça Vila de Madrid, shopping is in Barcelona's blood. Stretch your credit limit further by timing your trip to coincide with the sales (*rebaixes*), which generally run from the second week in January to the end of February, and throughout July and August, when prices are slashed by 50 per cent. In Barcelona, most shops (except department and convenience stores) tend to open Monday to Saturday, from 10am to 2pm, and – following a languid lunch – start reopening around 4.30pm until 8pm. (See p.142.)

Top of the Shops

El Corte Inglés

Plaça de Catalunya 14–16   93 306 38 00   www.elcorteingles.es
Mon–Sat 10am–10pm   Metro: Catalunya

Spain's favourite and only true department store, offering everything from gas cookers to groceries under one roof. Though it's a fair way from a thrilling shopping experience, a leisurely stroll around a few of the nine floors will give something of an insight into local life. Like department stores everywhere, the fashion sections will leave most readers of this guide cold, pitched at cardigan-wearers rather than

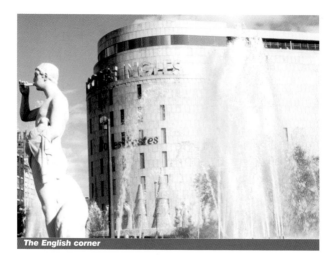

The English corner

trendsetters. The souvenir shop is best approached with irony.

However, it is particularly strong on sportswear, there's a superb electronics floor where you can fiddle with the latest MP3 players, and the men's underwear section is a revelation. If you can't find Calvins in your size or colour, there are racks of natty Spanish designs like Punto Blanco to tempt you instead. Similarly, the ground-floor perfumery is well stocked with unfamiliar local scents to intrigue a jaded nostril.

El Corte Ingléses are two-a-cent in Barcelona – there's another a minute's walk along Portal de l'Àngel – but this one is a landmark. Eating up a whole block of Plaça de Catalunya, it sits like a majestic white ocean liner in an Art Deco poster (though the façade was actually remodelled in 1994). Even if you're not buying, the views from the 9th-floor Rotonda restaurant across the city are hard to beat – and a great place to down a coffee and recharge.

Zara

ⓘ A. Pelai 58 📞 93 301 09 78
www.zara.com Ⓜ Metro: Catalunya

The ubiquitous, world-dominating Spanish chain that knocks out catwalk 'fakes' for the masses in record time – from drawing board to shop floor in a matter of weeks – needs no introduction. And especially not in this city, where it's seemingly not against the law – unwritten gay fashion law, that is –

to venture out in public dressed from head to toe in Zara.

The styles, cuts and quality of the clothes are the same as back home – so it's still three washes and you're out – but with up to 30 per cent off UK prices, who's complaining? It does, however, pay to be careful where you buy. The busy flagship on Passeig de Gràcia (No. 245) can be a no-go area at times, so this light, airy, well-stocked store, is a comparative sanctuary.

El Triangle

🛈 A. Pelai 39   📞 93 318 01 08
www.eltriangle.es   Ⓜ Metro: Catalunya

The hulking, visually non-descript mall opposite the El Corte Inglés on Plaça de Catalunya is relatively shy about its merits. Though bland and air-conditioned to the point of sterility, there's something commendably un-high street about its selection of middlebrow shops.

Start at the bottom in Sephora, the largest perfumery in the world. Entry is along a red sloped and mirrored runway that's part catwalk, part gauntlet – either way, a trial of nerves. Once in, it's always teeming with shoppers spritzing themselves with the testers; the written profiles describing the notes in each fragrance are a hoot. Engage one of the shop assistants in conversation and you could walk out with armfuls of free samples.

Come up to ground level for air. Here there are inoffensive mainstream fashions from the likes of Agatha, Dockers, Camper (walls of the quintessential Catalan deck shoe and variations on that theme), Massimo Dutti (for contemporary and fitted men's workwear), and Desigual, a unisex fashion outlet with borderline-outrageous printed gear. Also noteworthy is the FNAC, whose strongest suits are its CD, book and magazine departments, complete with the latest English-language publications.

El Triangle

Escribà Confiteria i Fleca

🛈 La Rambla 83
📞 93 301 60 27
Ⓜ Metro: Liceu

It's the remarkable blue Modernista mosaic covering the shop front that first attracts the eye – the windows of this dazzling corner bakery are filled with sweet delights – but it's the trays of glistening chocolates and cakes that drags you over the threshold. The Escribà Confiteria i Fleca is a one-stop choc stop-off for those on their way to pastry heaven, and the famous resident patissier, Antoni Escribà, could build a stairway to it out of meringue or chou, so heady are his towering confections shaped like world landmarks. As you're filling a box with goodies to take back to the hotel or scoff on a bench on the Rambla, ask to see the latest masterpiece he's working on out the back.

For an even better reason to stop by and blow the diet, there's a café at the rear. And if the waistline says you should stay away, beware: the team also run Xiringuitó Escribà, a remarkable seafront restaurant near the gay beach. (See p.56.)

ALL SHOPPED OUT

Vinçon

ⓘ Passeig de Gràcia 96 ☎ 93 215 60 50 www.vincon.com ◷ Mon–Sat
10am–8.30pm Ⓜ Metro: Diagonal

OK, so you might not be in Barcelona to buy a new dining suite or a
dinky bookcase for the spare room, but sometimes you've got to go
beyond Elle Déco to piece together a new look. And no place does
inspiring Catalan interiors quite as well as Vinçon, the city's most stylish
home outfitters.

Naturally enough, it's full of well-heeled gay couples ignoring the
designer brats springing on the mattresses in the bedding section. Done up
like a moody black-walled art gallery, presumably to justify the top-rung
prices as much as to give you an idea of how icons of 21st-century design
might look once you get the flatpack home, this showroom of style is a
one-off. Still, you could always take back a desirable picture frame, a set of
nibble bowls or an interesting corkscrew (made in Denmark, probably) as a
memento of your trip to the design city.

Ovlas

ⓘ Via Laietana 33 ☎ 93 268 76 91 ◷ Mon–Sat 10.30am–9pm Ⓜ Metro: Jaume I

Just round the corner from the Cathedral La Seu is – holy of holies – an
emporium dedicated to in-your-face gaywear. The gear here is own-label,
complete with rainbow-tag branding, and much of it carries a distinct
whiff of SM. This is where the gay underground look goes overground.
There's loads of black leather and PVC, but it's worth stocking up on
T-shirts here as they come in every colour, size and fit.

Though the glass-fronted boutique is unapologetically high street, the
beary staff plays up the menaces. But that doesn't deter nervous

heterosexual couples
popping in to look for
a kinkier than usual
piece to wear to the
club or in the bed-
room. It's full of gear
for special occasions
rather than wardrobe
staples, and its designs
are playful and just
about wearable – like
the jeans with tracksuit
edging. Once you've
seen the size of the bill
you've just run up,
you'll need a stiff drink
at the on-site café-bar.

Ovlas

Shop Around

FASHIONWEAR

ANTONI MIRÓ

A. Consell de Cent 349

93 487 06 70

www.antoniomiro.es

Metro: Passeig de Gràcia

Toni Miró is to Catalans what Jean-Paul Gaultier is to the French – their local designer-done-so-good that every gay Barcelonan wants him in their wardrobe. He's your scissorsmith if high-quality, off-the-peg contemporary menswear in that muted Mediterranean palette – black, beige and cream – is your look.

PURIFICACION GARCIA

Passeig de Gracia 22

93 487 72 92

www.purificaciongarcia.es

Metro: Passeig de Gracia

Metro Renowned for twists – sometimes literal – on classic items (diagonal cords anyone?), Purificacion Garcia will always come up with a must-have item in a colour you hadn't quite thought of on yourself. Slick, sleek and funky with prices a little above average, Garcia is already something of a Spanish fashion legend.

BAD HABITS

C. de Valencia 261

93 487 22 59 Metro: Passeig de Gràcia

Still doing the gypsy look? There's plenty of loose-legged, high-volume and nicely embroidered pieces on the racks at this favourite of ethereal, Mother Earth lesbians. Mind your head as you go down the steps on your way in.

COOL HUNTER

Passatge del Duc de la Victoria 5 93 302 37 78

Metro: Liceu

A small and oh-so stylish, in-the-know emporium sparsely stocked with pieces from the more exclusive, edgier Eurochic designers: DSquared, Vivienne Westwood and Dries Van Noten.

SUITE

C. Verdi 3–5

93 210 02 47

www.martargustems.com

Metro: Fontana

It's a bit out of the way for this foxy collection of cool new Spanish designers but well worth checking out, not only for fashion-forward menswear but for some quirky little designer knick-knacks that might make a good gift.

ALL SHOPPED OUT

CUSTO BARCELONA

🛈 Plaça de les Olles 6
📞 93 268 78 93
Ⓜ Metro: Jaume I

The high-fashion label that's a favourite with the stylists at *Shangay* magazine, judging from its appearance in almost every fashion story. Designer Custodio Dalmau's exclusive boutique in the Born district has the craziest patterned tops, psychedelic long-sleeved tops and body-hugging sweaters.
For show-offs who like to make an entrance.

DIESEL

🛈 Corner of Passeig de Gràcia and A Diputació
📞 93 445 83 64
Ⓜ Metro: Passeig de Gràcia

It's a staple in every gay and lesbian wardrobe, and all your favourite lines are here (although no cheaper than at home). But should you fancy your nth piece of Diesel denim, you'll be glad you popped by.

KWATRA

🛈 A. Antic de Sant Joan 1
📞 93 268 08 04
www.kwatra.com
Ⓜ Metro: Jaume I

The first unibrand store in Spain – in the cutting-edge Born district, naturally enough – selling the coolest Nikes, with carefully selected tops and bottoms from of-the-moment names that mix and match to complement the footwear.

LACOSTE

🛈 Rambla Catalunya 72
📞 93 487 1527
Ⓜ Metro: Catalunya

A belatedly gay label from France – something to do with that poster campaign with a naked male model – the store in Barcelona stocks

Diesel time

designs exclusive to Catalonia. Drop by to pick up an oh-so-now polo shirt.

SO_DA

ⓘ A. de Avinyó 24
☎ 93 412 27 76
Ⓜ Metro: Liceu

One of the trendiest streets in the Barri Gòtic, limited editions rule. The only place in Barcelona to find the diaphanous designs of, say, Stella McCartney *and* Yohji Yamamoto's Adidas strap-up fashion boot. At night, the collections are locked away and the doors flung open for fashion happenings, with DJ sets and cocktails.

TRIBU

ⓘ C. Avinyo 12
☎ 93 318 65 10
Ⓜ Metro: Jaume I

If you're looking for something hot to go out in tonight, you might just find the right T-shirt or designer trainer in this little treasure chest of a boutique featuring everything from [cool] global brands to names you've never heard of.

SECOND-HAND GEAR

RECICLA RECICLA

ⓘ A. Riera Baixa 13

Antinous . . .

☎ 93 443 18 15
Ⓜ Metro: Sant Antoni

Where dedicated followers of flea-market fashion rummage alongside fans of Sergio Tacchini originals.

MIES I FELJ

ⓘ A. Riera Baixa 5
☎ 93 442 07 55
Ⓜ Metro: Liceu

Large and well-ordered selection of second-hand denim, with Levis a speciality.

MUSIC AND BOOKS

ANTINOUS

ⓘ A. Josep Anselm Clavé 6
☎ 93 301 90 70
www.antinouslibros.com
Ⓜ Metro: Drassanes

A thoughtful, contemporary lesbian and gay bookshop in Barri Gòtic, which doubles as an information centre. Run by quietly

dedicated staff (who'll give you the lowdown on gay Barcelona), it's a great place to browse – there's a small selection of English-language books – and occasional events in the café. But the biggest thumbs-up is for the stock of gay magazines and listings guides.

DISCOS BALADA

ⓘ A. Pelai 24
Ⓜ Universitat,Catalunya

This bargain-basement CD store can be a hit-and-miss affair, but it often throws up the occasional gem. It pays to dig: as well as the latest chart releases, there are always absurdly low offers on back catalogue CDs – anyone for a long-forgotten Prince 3-CD set for €5? – plus great box sets and an interesting classical selection.

FNAC

See El Triangle (p.61).

Head for La Boqueria

EL CORTE INGLÉS

ℹ Portal de l'Àngel 19
☎ 93 306 38 00
Ⓜ Metro: Catalunya

Comprehensive ground-floor CD and DVD department at the satellite of the nearby flagship branch in Plaça Catalunya (See pp.59–60.)

HOME INTERIORS

DOM

ℹ C. Provença 249–251
☎ 93 487 11 81
www.id-dom.com
Ⓜ Metro: Passeig de Gracia

Barcelona is full of middlebrow interior shops selling superior home décor. The buyer at this one has the well-to-do homo-at-home in mind. It's also presided over by pretty-boy assistants who seem to enjoy giving gay customers a knowing look. If you don't want to walk out with a fun plastic shower curtain, wire magazine rack or a nest of moulded perspex tables, there's also a selection of rare imported chillout CDs which you can sample before you buy.

MARKETS

ELS ENCANTS

See p.27.

SWEET THINGS

ENRIC ROVIRA

ℹ A Josep Tarradellas 113
☎ 93 419 25 47
www.enricrovira.com
Ⓜ Metro: Entença

There's no shortage of posh chocolatiers in Barcelona, where many of them come in an olde-worlde style. But Enric Rovira brings things right up to date without throwing any tasty babies out with the bathwater. Pick up some great gifts, like a Gaudi Passeig de Gracia paving stone in chocolate or some turrones in a variety of flavours though the basic almond one is favourite – and don't let them tell you it's just for Christmas: it's great after dinner.

GAY SHOPS

NOSTROMO

ℹ C. Diputacio 208
☎ 93 451 33 23
Ⓜ Metro: Universitat

A great gay sex shop that goes the extra mile, putting on special events for Gay Pride and providing a fully authorised cruising zone including video cabins with extra surprises.

SESTIENDA

ℹ A. Rauric 11   ☎ 93 318 86 76 www.sestienda.com
Ⓜ Metro: Urgell

One of Barcelona's first sex shops, still giving good, discreet service. There are plenty of booths for you to fast-forward through your selection of vids before deciding.

ZEUS

ℹ A. Riera Alta 20
☎ 93 442 97 95
Ⓜ Metro: Sant Antoni

Slightly awkwardly located sex shop stuck in a busy immigrant area of the Raval. Still, a great place to pop in for a browse or to pick up a gay listings mag.

SHOPPING MALLS

MAREMÀGNUM

ℹ Moll d'Espanya, Port Vell
☎ 93 225 81 00
www.maremagnum.es
Ⓜ Metro: Barceloneta

The smoked and mirrored glass exterior of this monolithic mall complex on the port edge shrouds little mystery inside. It's the predictable run of uninspiring low-rent clothing stores, family or theme restaurants and tourist tat shops.

Time for tapas

Eating Out

Barcelona eats late. Unless you enjoy being first into restaurants or dining alone, synchronise your stomach rumbles with the Catalan clock. Lunch is an unhurried affair, soaking up the hours between 2 and 4pm (and then it's siesta, so plenty of time for another coffee…), while dinner is served no earlier than 9pm (and often at midnight). Around 6pm, the city decamps to a *granja* for a pastry pick-me-up and milky hot drink, or to a tapas bar for something quick on a stick over a beer.

Visitors are pleasantly surprised by how easy it is to eat well and cheaply in Barcelona. Lunch is better value still if you ask for the *menú del día* (menu of the day) rather than ordering à la carte. For a choice of several starters, entrées, a dessert, bread and a drink, expect to get change from €10. Barcelona's foodie scene is as internationalist as the city itself.

Cream of the Cuisine

Castro

ℹ C. Casanova 85
📞 93 323 67 84
🕑 Mon–Fri 1pm–4pm, 9pm–midnight; Sat 9pm–midnight 🚇 Metro: Urgell
🍴 🍴

Gay restaurants come no more elegant than this – though there's not a frilly tablecloth in sight, and the only jacket required is a leather one. The décor is industrial chic, the walls are charcoal and gun-grey, with

The following price guides have been used for eating out and indicate the price for a main course:

🍴 = cheap = under €7

🍴 = moderate = €7–€17

🍴 = expensive = over €17

concrete columns wrapped with chains – imagine dining in a softly-lit sex dungeon – and the sense of theatre palpable: once coats are taken, they are handcuffed to the stand. The serious, black T-shirted staff, with their regimented authority and inside-out knowledge of the menu, add to the sub-dom atmosphere.

But this is no S&M theme restaurant – it's one of the best places to eat in town. Accordingly, there's a mix of dining gourmets (though most are moustachioed), and all are smart but not stuffily dressed for the occasion; put on your best leather trews for a night here. In spite of the upmarket sleaze feel, it's not so much a gay restaurant as a restaurant that's gay. The ingenious menu sparkles.

Warm rolls and *fuet* (spicy Catalan sausage) come as cover, and there's an impressive prix fixe with four choices for each course. For starters, the *sopa fría* (chilled soup) is like frothy milk laced with melon chunks; the carpaccio is well paired with pear and nuts.

The playful Catalan spirit is much in evidence in the main course selection; the grilled veg platter comes with courgette, carrot, pineapple and kiwi in the skins and rind – an excellent surprise (though rather dented by the undersized portion). Carnivores might like the pork with goat's cheese.

The service is defiantly not flappy, but competent and helpful. Ask for assistance with the wine list, a toss-up between the local reds from Penedès.

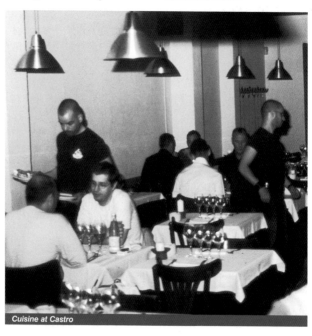

Cuisine at Castro

Jaume de Provença

ℹ️ C. Provença 88 📞 93 430 00 29 🍴 Tues–Sat 1pm–4pm, 9pm–11.15pm, Sun 1pm–4pm 🚇 Metro: Entença 🍴 🛏️

With the décor time-locked in the 1970s – and not in a knowing, tongue-in-cheek retro way – fads in Catalan cuisine have washed over this Gràcia bolt-hole (est. 1942), which teeters on the edge of fashionability by being resolutely impervious to its swings and roundabouts. In keeping with the height of the prawn-cocktail-years ambience, the menu champions 'market cooking' and is typified by good old steak and mushrooms (albeit wild ceps). It's a good place to splash out for a mini-celebration with friends – the *menu degustation* kicks off with a cleansing avocado cappuccino, and includes house specialities like pork trotters, lobster and rosemary roasted lamb. There's also a cheaper menu of supposed seasonal Catalan goodies that proves the local kitchen's magpie tendencies, as it includes *bacalão con all-i-oli de mangos* (strips of cod done Basque country style, served with mango mayo) and *mousaka de conejo confitado* (rabbit moussaka). A la carte mains start at €15 and promptly rocket – as do prices on the decent wine list.

Botafumeiro

ℹ️ Gran de Gràcia 81 📞 93 218 42 30 🍴 Daily 1pm–1am 🚇 Metro: Fontana 🍴 🛏️

Seafood fans take note: this is widely considered the best restaurant for fish in town – as the waiting list attests. If it swims, you're pretty much guaranteed to be able to eat it here, served up in typical Galician (rather than Catalan) style. With a restaurant of this size – some 300 covers set out impeccably in a Baroque banqueting hall – and an international reputation to live up to, the waiters in gold-trim white uniforms are drilled for their part in what amounts to a nightly military manoeuvre; service can border on the brisk and intrusive. But come here for the menu, not the table-side manner. Specialities include oysters, lobster and langoustines – which you can earmark from a tank of dozens – as well as fish and meat stews. The enormous list of Galician white wines begs to be sampled.

if you prefer, the takeaways are substantial

Seltz

ⓘ C. Rossellò 154 **☎** 93 453 60 99
🕐 Wed–Sat 9pm–3am
Ⓜ Metro: Hospital Clínic 🍴 🍸

This vermouth bar is at the vanguard of a club-cum-restaurant trend that has swept Barcelona: think of it as a dancerie-eaterie. Have an aperitif at the counter, then as the DJ warms up, try some trendy tapas from the select menu of *platitos*, small side dishes of the chef's own invention. And when the tables are cleared away, dance it all off to hard house. Definitely a concept not to be missed – and the illuminated frosted flooring decorated with Campari labels is very Saturday Night Fever.

La Flauta Magica

ⓘ C. de Banys Vells 18 **☎** 93 268 46 94
🕐 Wed–Mon 9pm–midnight, closed Tues
Ⓜ Metro: Jaume I 🍴 🍸

A loudly decorated boho hangout in Born, popular with a hardcore trustafarian element who read out scenes from their latest screenplays at the recital nights every Thursday. While not strictly meat-free (its cuts are organic), it has some of the choicest veggie platters, which draw inspiration from the world over. The mushroom crêpe is a winner, and the sushi on the picture menu (served at weekends only) looks inviting. Will you be joining the in-crowd for Sri Lankan curried rice or corn fritters from Venezuela?

Jupiter

ⓘ C. Jupi 4 **☎** 93 268 36 50 www.jupiteryluna.com **🕐** Tues–Thur, Sun 7pm–1am; Fri–Sat 7pm–2am **Ⓜ** Metro: Jaume I 🍴 🍸

This place is a nightmare to find, hidden in a seedy backstreet off Via Laietana at the back of the main post office, but, wow, what a find! A gay-run left-field lounge restaurant popular with manga-comic reading grungers, the décor gives a good indication of the playfully inventive menu that

awaits. There are bamboo decorations on the walls, a chill-out bit with reconditioned settees and 70s coffee tables – and a main eating area. *Bocadillos* and salads provide the main ballast to the nibble-friendly menu, and no dish is more than €10. The portions are small and satisfying, which makes it easy to try as many dishes as you can from the extensive list.

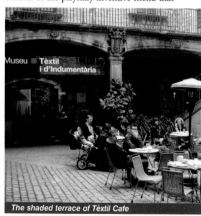

The shaded terrace of Tèxtil Cafe

Café Miranda

ⓘ C. Casanova 30
☎ 93 453 52 49
⏱ Tues–Sun 9pm–1am
Ⓜ Metro: Universitat 🍴 🏆

Barcelona's first drag restaurant, this sister to the flagship (dragship?) in Madrid has been packing them in ever since it opened its velvet drape-covered doors. The professional cabaret performers (drag queens, dancers, acrobats and even trapeze artists) do their best to detain you from your meal with their high-octane, highly polished routines. There's such a buzz about the place, and it's a fixture both in the gay listings mags and the reviews pages of local papers, so straight diners also flock here for a kitsch night out. Secure a table well in advance, especially at weekends when last-minute bookings will have the accommodating front desk pulling their (own) hair out.

Tèxtil Cafe

ⓘ C. Montcada 12 ☎ 93 268 25 98
⏱ Tues–Sat 10am– 6pm, Sun 10am–3pm Ⓜ Metro: Jaume I 🍴 🏆

Madrid-Barcelona

Madrid-Barcelona

ⓘ C. d'Aragó 282 ⏱ Mon–Sat 1pm–3.30pm, 8.30pm–11.30pm
☎ 93 215 70 27 Ⓜ Metro: Passeig de Gràcia 🍴 🏆

Most nights of the week, especially weekends, and even during lunch, there are patient queues outside this 1920s marisco bar located on the old Madrid to Barcelona railway line (it was part of the former station). Appropriately, the menu is a fusion of Spanish and Catalan favourites, though the *pa amb tomàquet* (bread rubbed with tomato, a Catalan speciality) served with steamed mussels and chunky fish soup gets the juices flowing fastest.

This smart courtyard café at the Museu Tèxtil i d'Indumentària has plenty to recommend it. The cool, shaded terrace is dressed with conservatory furniture, offers great veggie options – there's a whole page in the menu devoted to meat-free mains, and plenty of starters to weigh up, too – but here's the deal-clincher: expect to pay €20 per head for three courses, coffee and a brandy or two. Shamelessly geared towards tourists, it falls shy of pulling in coach-loads of the baseball-capped masses, but it's something of a highlight in one of the Barri Gòtic's most popular attractions. Try a comforting 'taste of home' plate containing typical Spanish, Italian, Lebanese, Japanese (and so on) fare, or sandwiches named after the cities associated with the fillings, like a pastrami and rye (New York) and London's BLT (or bacon, lettuce and tomato). In fact, its only major downside is that it's not open late enough for dinner – unless your stomach has yet to acclimatise to continental meal times.

Best of the Rest

Bracafé

BRACAFÉ
🛈 C. de Casp 2
🕿 93 302 30 82
⏲ Open 7am–10.30pm
daily 🚇 Catalunya
🍴 🍸 Cash only

An always-crammed
Brazilian coffee bar
with amazing Art Deco
fittings and possibly the
strongest brews in
town. Grab a table in
the street, just off
Passeig de Gràcia.
Mind those shopping
bags, though…

CASA CALVET
🛈 C. de Casp 48
🕿 93 412 40 12
⏲ Mon–Sat 1pm–3.30pm,
8.30pm–11pm 🚇 Metro:
Urquinaona 🍴 🍸

Set in the gorgeous
interiors of Antonio
Gaudí's first
commissioned
apartment building in
Barcelona, this ought
to be a tourist trap; it's
the only place in town
where you can eat
inside a Modernista
landmark. But its
enduring reputation for
fine Catalan/
Mediterranean with a
twist has been secured
by the elegant setting
and local inventive
favourites such as
oyster ravioli dressed
with foamy Cava-laced
sauce.

CAL PEP
🛈 C. de les Olles 8
🕿 93 310 79 61
⏲ Mon 8pm–11.30pm,
Tues–Sat 1pm–4.30pm,
8.30pm–11.30pm. Closed
Aug. 🚇 Barceloneta 🍴
🍸

Antiquated fish joint
that's lorded over by a
convivial owner.
Popular with hardy
Barceloneta locals, who
sup on the best fruits of
the sea caught that day.

LA VERÓNICA
🛈 C. Avinyó 30
🕿 93 412 11 22
⏲ Tues 8pm–1.30am,
Wed–Sun noon–1.30am
🚇 Metro: Jaume I 🍴 🍸

Radical pizzeria with
blonde wood tables and
a loud paint job, where
lipstick lesbians come
to hold court over a
wild mushroom salad
or two.

ANTIGUA CASA SOLÉ
🛈 C. Sant Carles 4
🕿 93 221 50 12
⏲ Closed Sunday nights
and Mondays 🚇 Metro:
Barceloneta 🍴 🍸

For seafood that cries out to be photographed as well as a treat to eat. Book yourself in for a languid Sunday afternoon lunch of *arroç negre amb sepia en su tinta* (literally, 'black rice with squid in its own ink').

GOVINDA

ℹ️ Plaça de la Vila de Madrid 4–5

📞 93 318 77 29

🕐 Mon–Thur 1pm–4pm, 8pm–11pm; Fri–Sat 1pm–4pm, 8pm–11.45pm

Ⓜ️ Metro: Catalunya

🍴 💶

Veggie Indian with weekly changing menu of *paneers, dhals, koftas* and *Bengali sabji* – with occasional screwball options like enchiladas to remind you that you're in Spain. There's also a well-replenished salad bar.

COMME BIO

ℹ️ Gran Via de les Corts Catalanes 603

📞 93 301 03 76

🕐 Mon–Sat 8am–10.30pm; Sun & public holidays noon–10.30pm

Ⓜ️ Metro: Passeig de Gràcia

🍴 💶

A vegeterian botega with an inspiring way with textured proteins like tofu. Great salad starters, and the killer main is the risotto marina made with tofu, seaweed and smoky ceps. It's pricy, the décor's not up to much, and waiters are unrushable and on the dopey side. A minor find for grateful health foodists.

TENORIO

ℹ️ Passeig de Gràcia 37

📞 93 272 05 92/94

🕐 Daily noon–1.30am

Ⓜ️ Metro: Passeig de Gràcia 🍴 💶

Swish and stylish are the passwords at this international brasserie for the designer shopping fraternity. This place is power-dressed straight out of the 80s (that's Catalan irony for you). There's purple dark wood and chrome everywhere, lit large by enormous arc lights. If that's too much theatre, snag a table on the terrace, where prim portions are served on frosted glass plate-bowls.

TRAGALUZ

ℹ️ Passatge de la Concepció 5

📞 93 487 06 21

🕐 Mon–Wed, Sun 1.30pm–4pm, 8.30pm–midnight; Thur–Sat 1.30pm–4pm, 8.30pm–1am

Ⓜ️ Metro: Diagonal

🍴 💶

Tucked in an Eixample side street, this colourful resto-bar with a planet-arium-like glass roof is great for fine, informal dining – and stargazing. The *menu degustation* comes at a fairly reasonable price, or for simple finger food choose between club

International cuisine

sandwiches, hamburgers and fajitas. There's a good veggie selection, too. All the fittings here are designed by Javier Mariscal, creator of 1992 Olympic mascot, Cobi.

LA DIVA RESTAURANT

🛈 C. Diputació 172
📞 93 454 63 98
🕐 Mon–Sun 9pm–midnight; show at 11pm (Thur–Sun)
🚇 Metro: Universitat
🍴 🎫 Mon–Wed €20, Thurs–Sun €27. Booking essential

Another drag restaurant – Barcelona foodies love their 'amuse girls' – the pretender to Café Miranda's throne. Come for the show, rather than the food.

LA SINGULAR

🛈 C. Francisco Giner
📞 93 237 50 98
🕐 From 8pm (closed Sundays)
🚇 Metro: Fontana 🍴 🎫

Where the girls are. Swinging lesbian-run and owned restaurant in Gràcia, which packs them in. Good international food, great, warm ambience.

TOMATE

🛈 C. dels Sombreres 17

🕐 Tues–Sun 10am–midnight, closed Mon
📞 93 315 1048 🚇 Metro: Jaume I 🍴 🎫

A neat cucina vegetariana in the Barri Gòtic where you eat surrounded by lotus lampshades and pictures of Vishnu. The unbeatable lunchtime buffet and salad bar costs next to nothing.

GRANJA M VIADER

🛈 C. Xuclà 4–6
📞 93 318 34 86
🕐 Mon 5pm–8.45pm; Tues–Sat 9am–1.45pm, 5pm–8.45pm; closed 2 weeks in Aug 🚇 Metro: Catalunya 🍴 🎫

Well-to-do *granja* bar packed with Catalan ladies with good hairdos and their pipe-smoking partners. Part of Barcelona's fabric, the original owners' medals are proudly displayed around the walls, alongside reviews from newspapers through the ages.

CAFÉ TORINO

🛈 Passeig de Gràcia 59
📞 93 487 75 77
🕐 Mon–Thur, Sun 8am–11pm; Fri, Sat 9am–1.30am
🚇 Metro: Passeig de Gràcia 🍴 🎫 Cash only

Popular corner café bar in the Eixample,

Popular corner café bar

with a striking curved-beamed entrance. A handy stop-off when doing the Modernista sights on Passeig de Gràcia.

AMALTEA

🛈 C. Diputació 164
📞 93 454 86 13
🕐 Mon–Thur 9am–10pm; Fri-Sat 9am–midnight; closed Sun 🚇 Metro: Urgell 🍴 🎫

Deli-front café in the Gaixample with a great veggie *menú del día* for peanuts.

EL FORTUNY

🛈 C. Pintor Fortuny 31
📞 93 317 98 92
🕐 Tues–Sun 10am–1.30am 🚇 Metro: Catalunya 🍴 🎫 Cash only

Perfect for a quiet sit and smoke as you wait for your unfussy home-cooked meal to arrive. A popular lesbian bodega, stacked with old barrels and funkily decorated with toy robots, though you still get the odd elderly gent walking in for the dinner, too.

RESTAURANT FINDER

Local drink, Cava

As you eat your way through mountains of fresh fruits of the sea and other delights from the Barcelona kitchen, think: what to wash it down with? The answer is cava, the Catalans' response to champagne. This sparkling white wine is aged in underground cellars (*cava* means cellar in Catalan), and is drunk by the glass to celebrate no occasion whatsoever; treat yourself to a glass first in the early evening. Sipping a chilled flute is as common here as

pint – downing is in London – and it's a good look for gay bars. Look out for Freixenet and its long-time rival Codorniu – or head for a pre-clubbing tipple with the trendies at El Xampanyet, a buzzing Cava palace.

Cava – celebrate life

EL XAMPANYET
🛈 C. Montcada 22
📞 93 319 70 03 🕐 Daily
6.30pm–11.30pm Ⓜ Jaume I

SALVATION
GAY DISCO

music bar
EFLEJOS

ra. 19   Sitges

LE MALE A BAR

CENTRO
COMERCIAL
OASIS
LOCAL

Out on the Town

So Barcelona hasn't got the biggest scene in the world, or even in Spain – that's one distinction that goes to Madrid and its gay village, Chueca. And variety isn't the spice of gay life here, either. The upmarket style bars in the Left Eixample, or Gaixample, are often high-concept variations on a well-shaken cocktail: a young, trendy crowd, designer décor and €5 plus for a spirit and a bottle of mixer.

But the city has plenty for gay partygoers to write home about, not least its attitude – or rather the lack of it. Less up itself than London and New York, the vibe is fashion-conscious but come-as-you-are, to the extent that gays and lesbians happily welcome each other into their bars (the boys are mostly in Gaixample; the girls congregate in Gràcia). Some of the gayest hangouts – like the after-hours clubs (after 6am) – aren't officially gay, but you wouldn't know from all that hugging…

My Top Clubs

Metro

 C. Sepúlveda 185 93 323 52 27 www.metrodiscobcn.com Daily midnight–6am Metro: Universitat €10 (plus free drink). Free passes handed out at Café Dietrich

In a town where what's hot changes with every issue of *Nois* magazine, Metro is a rare institution, impervious to the whims of fashion and packing them in with its formula of unpretentious pop you can bop to, even if it has recently been renovated. Whether they like to admit it or not, it's every boy's favourite club. The main dance floor is a hands–aloft mix of current hits from the European and American charts, while the second delves into the disco archives – but not too far back; Las Ketchup's

OUT ON THE TOWN

Asereje is guaranteed to be played nightly, while it's not unknown for full-blown sevillanas – family party flamenco – to break out. Ricochet between the two floors as soon as you can – once the place picks up at 3am, it'll be so busy you won't want to move around. Clubbing doesn't come any sweatier than this.

Need a rest? There's chilling out to be had around the pool table, and there's always plenty of queues to join. Those for the gents' toilets are legendary: perhaps it's something to do with the monitors above the urinals that play porn on a loop… Midweek drag shows pull in a boisterous mixed crowd, and look out for the occasional foam parties, which are also legendary. Thanks to an unimaginably confusing layout, many a lost clubber has also been known to stumble upon the spacious darkroom and porn chamber. Whatever you're into, Metro is a must for the sheer fun factor alone. Don't leave town without trying it.

Dietrich

ⓘ C. Consell de Cent 255

☏ 93 451 77 07 **🕐** Daily 6pm–2.30am (Sat 3am) **Ⓜ** Universitat

As the name suggests, the city's most famous gay bar has a slight German accent. The first thing you'll notice, waltzing past the bouncers and through dramatic thick red drapes, is the enormous cartoon portrait of Marlene, striking her classic pose, but haggard to the point of grotesqueness, her pendulous, age-withered carriage grazing her knees. *Wilkommen*, as they say, to Barcelona's tongue-in-cheek taste of Berlin.

It may be past its first flush of youth but style is the name of the game here, a mix of contemporary beige and Art Deco fittings strewn with giant plants. There's a narrow slipway lined with mirrors and stools – perfect for hanging with a drink while pretending not to be taking a good look at new arrivals. The long, L-shaped bar, which is watched over by an attractive T-shirted crew who have among their ranks some of the most attentive servers in town, leads to a raised dance floor at the back. Dietrich is all about getting in the mood to move on elsewhere, so there's a rosta of DJs on deck duty, getting the party started. But that's only the half of it.

This being Barcelona, the dance area is intermittently cleared for drag performers to mouth their way through mini routines. And this being Dietrich, the entertainment goes that little bit further than the local norm. Throughout the night, go-go boys dance on whatever podiums they can make available, while the occasional fire-breathing circus act wows the crowds in the ornamental garden. Or maybe you'd prefer a Tina Turner marionette show!

You don't go out in Barcelona without stopping by Dietrich first. And it's worth popping in for the free passes to Metro. On Friday nights it's full of new faces, lads (and the occasional lass) from all over the continent, straight off the plane, getting busy chatting each other up in Spanish, French, Dutch or whatever. Now that's the kind of European union Marlene would approve of.

The famous Dietrich

Punto BCN

ⓘ C. Muntaner 63
☎ 93 453 61 23
☾ Mon–Sat 6pm–2.30am, Sun 6pm–3am
Ⓜ Metro: Universitat

Like La Rambla, during a trip to Barcelona you will end up in Punto at some point – usually sooner rather than later. For this is the early bird's bar of choice.

Anyone who's out for the night rocks up here for their first drink of the evening – which is everyone from the slew of tight T-shirted disco bunnies who stream in constantly, to the older, pipe-smoking men in cardigans with dogs on leads who never seem to arrive or leave. All types in between are invited, too – and

happily that also includes women. Though it's a boys' bar, there's always a healthy flow of lesbians, as well as a few straight girls in tow (wherever those disco bunnies go…).

One of the first heavy-hitting bars on the block to open, it's cavernous, airy, and with air con so strong it could snuff a match. The look is unthreateningly anodyne – Americana meets Eurostyle – with a long bar decorated with Budweiser ads, Coke ads and Molson neons. Though there's enough floor space for an army of friends, it fills quickly, making it an easy spot for strangers looking to look inconspicuous. If you are on your own, hang back by the mini art gallery, and before long you'll be engaged in conversation.

Alternatively, hang round the pool table upstairs.

As Punto is run by the same group as the Arena clubs (which are predominantly heterosexual nowadays), with every drink you'll be handed discount flyers. A better bet, free passes to Salvation disco are handed out at about 1.30am on Fridays and Saturdays.

Bright decor at Átame bar. (See p.86)

Salvation

🛈 Ronda Sant Pere, 19–21   📞 93 318 06 86 www.matineegroup.com   🗓 Fri–Sat and festival days midnight–5am   Ⓜ Metro: Urquinaona   💲 €10

The gay disco that all Barcelona wishes it could gatecrash. But despite being bang in the non-gay heart of the city, it's almost strictly men only. Only a handful of hand-picked female plus-ones are plucked from the long queues outside every night.

So what's the fuss about? First, there's an on-the-money aficionado's room for guest DJs playing quality dance, which is packed all night with gyrating bodies. And for those with less upscale musical tastes, there's an equally busy modern trash and retro floor with a fun line in

Europop. On Friday nights there are live spectaculars, but there's no getting away from the fact this is, basically, a slightly harder-core version of Metro. The magic's working, though – bouncers have been turning away straights since it first opened in 1999. It's worth hunting down the flyers which offer free entrance on Fridays, and reduced door damage on Saturdays and holidays.

Martins

🛈 Passeig de Gràcia, 130   📞 93 218 71 67 www.discomartins.com   🗓 Daily midnight–5am   Ⓜ Metro: Diagonal   💲 €8

This fabulous dinosaur is so old, the Gaixample didn't exist when it first opened at the 'wrong' end of Passeig de Gràcia some 20 years ago. (Back then, the Sagrada Família, a few blocks away, would have looked very different.) But it's easy to see why this cruisy ultra-late venue has not only survived, but thrived.

Impervious to the fickle finger of fashion, Martins is where men come to play, especially when nearby bars like the Eagle and New Chaps have chucked out for the night. The vibe is suitably heavy, reflected in the industrial, warehousey look. There's little by way of relief from the black painted walls, unless you count the one-way mirror in the gents' toilets which allows you to watch newcomers arrive as you stand at the urinal.

A late-night pick-up joint, there are dark areas and a loft playing porn on a big screen. Oh, there's also a dance floor for those who want it. On an off night, when it's not busy, it's easy to rattle around Martins, cavernous as it is. But hold out for the delegation of pneumatic transsexuals that inevitably, and inexplicably, arrive for a dance with the jackboot and leather fraternity. At Martins, everyone's welcome, tourists especially. Look out for flyers, which offer free entry until 4.30am.

G Café

ⓘ C. Muntaner 24
☎ No phone
🕓 Daily 7pm–3am
Ⓜ Metro: Universitat

The 'G' in the name is for 'gay',

and also for 'Gaudí'. Stands to reason, as God's architect has inspired the look and the vibe at this small but unique bar. Like its namesake, who was passionate in his attention to detail, the décor borders on the devotional. The bar itself looks like a Gaudí offcut, its coloured animal mosaics undulating like the benches in Park Güell. In contrast, the walls are stark white and hung with crucifixes, with church candles leaking wax over every table top. With the solemnity tempered by touches of Catholic kitsch, this place feels like a temple. This is the height of the alternative gay scene in Barcelona, and seems all the more outré for its flouting of the city's modern bar design conventions. Here, all the

Put your hands in the air

furniture is perversely odd, a hotchpotch of random dining chairs, chaise longues and armchairs in need of re-upholstering. Behind the bar, there's a small selection of drinks; the best spirits and the owner's favourite beer – which means it feels like you've been invited to a salon.

Open for civilised chilling during the afternoon siesta, when there's an easy soundtrack of well-chosen lounge compilations, at night it becomes a dance bar presided over by a low-key ambient DJ. Tables are simply pushed aside to make way. But whether you hit the floor or prefer to curl your feet up to relax, it's so informal, it's your prerogative. Out of the way on the outer limits of the Gaixample – but it's worth getting out the map to find.

Bear Factory

🛈 Ptge Domingo 3
www.bearfactorybarcelona.com
✷ Wed, Thur, Sun 11pm–3am;
Fri, Sat 11pm–5am
Ⓜ Metro: Universitat

It had to happen sooner or later. Barcelona has joined the international movement for those gentlemen fuzzy of face, chunky of waist to have their own attitude-free space to let their hair down and shake it all about. Bear Factory is it. And what a success it has been. A large bar dotted with bear business with dancing, regular parties (F★cktory is always rammed) and even strip shows, the brand is so successful - and not only with bears either! - that they have even branched out to host the first ever bear cruise. Expect a mixed crowd, fairly dressed down and ready for big fun and be prepared for a certain amount of sexual electricity, especially at those parties. Bears and bear-lovers should also check out Ursus Fenix (www.ursusplanet.com), a midweek meeting place at Casanova 64.

Z:eltas

🛈 C. Casanova 75
☎ 93 454 19 02 www.zeltas.net
✷ Daily 11pm–3am Ⓜ Metro: Urgell

The vibeyest, most fashion-conscious meeting point pulls in a dressy crowd of all ages and persuasions. The long, narrow bar – a riot of exposed brickwork, painted murals and plasma screens playing pop videos – is perfect for posing. Further along, it opens out into a dance area, which gets busy after 1am. If you're staying a while, it's worth checking your coat in at the back while there's still space.

Best described as a place for friends rather than friendly. The clientele can be on the cliquey side, although the smiley bar staff do their best to keep everyone happy. If you're waiting on your own, there are plenty of gay magazines to graze. Pull up a stool and nurse an enormous house measure, or slouch out on the cream sofas.

The bar feel gives way later to a clubbier vibe. Before you head off to Metro or Salvation, remember to take the flyers being handed out at the door, offering free passes to after-hours clubs. In Barcelona, you never know where a night will lead…

Gay T Dance

ℹ️ C. Tarragona 141–147
🌐 www.matineegroup.com
🕐 From 9pm Sun
Ⓜ️ Metro: Tarragona

This crazy night out used to be housed in the down-home old Apolo, which was well worth a look whatever the night, but has since been taken over and relocated and generally sorted out by the Matinee Group, the guys behind Salvation, arguably the hottest spot in town, and Space in Ibiza. At the time of writing the new GTD had not been launched but the team promised the new space (Space!) would see the club retain its masculinity and its imagination.

Clubbing scene

Aire

ℹ️ C. València 236 (between C. Balmes and C. Enriq Granados)
🌐 93 487 83 42
www.arenadisco.com
🕐 Thur–Sat 11.30pm–3am; Sun (women only) 6pm–10pm
Ⓜ️ Metro: Passeig de Gràcia
💲 €3 (Sat €6, includes one drink)

Barcelona's biggest and busiest lesbian venue pulls in more than 300 women most nights. Part of the Arena group (who also run Punto BCN (see pp.81–82), this is a suitably stylish and unpretentious girl dance bar. As the Saturday Night Fever coloured dance floor suggests, the parties here swing with sounds of the past, but there's enough contemporary pop and house thrown in to keep the more fashion-minded dyke happy. It's strictly women only on Sundays (there's even an early-evening strip show on the first Sunday of the month), though throughout the rest of the week men are welcome as guests.

Café de L'Opera

OUT ON THE TOWN

All Clubbed Out

AMBAR

- ℹ️ C. Casanova 71
- ☎️ 93 451 59 94
- 🌙 Daily 6pm–3am
- Ⓜ️ Metro: Universitat

All-day lounge bar, in the heart of the Gaixample, with chillout sounds until 11pm, then harder house until closing.

ARENA CLASSIC

- ℹ️ C. Diputació 233
- ☎️ 93 487 83 42
- www.arenadisco.web
- 🌙 Fri and Sat only 12.30pm–5am
- Ⓜ️ Metro: Universitat
- 🎟️ €5 Fri, €9 Sat

The best of the Arena group disco attracts a fun-loving crowd lapping up anthems from the 70s, 80s, 90s and right now, and gets cheesier as the night goes on. A refreshingly unpretentious mix of lesbians, gay men and mates makes this the ideal big Saturday night out for groups.

ÁTAME

- ℹ️ C. Consell de Cent 257
- ☎️ 93 454 92 73
- 🌙 6pm–2.30am, Fri–Sat 3am
- Ⓜ️ Metro: Universitat

A one–drink-then-move-on kind of place, with an odd mix of hustlers and couples engaged in intimate conversations.

BACKSY CAFÉ

- ℹ️ C. Diputació 161
- ☎️ 93 451 52 58
- 🌙 Daily 10am–2.30am
- Ⓜ️ Metro: Urgell

Straight-acting multi-screened video bar, with gorgeous barmen and screens everywhere playing a mix of terrestrial TV, football matches and gay porn. Magazine racks are stuffed with *Men's Health, Zeus* and the weekend supplements. Thursday happy hour 9–11pm, with two for one drinks. Breakfast and lunch also offered.

XT

- ℹ️ C. Diputacio 93
- 🌙 Wed–Fri; 9pm–3am, Sat–Sun 6am–10am
- Ⓜ️ Metro: Rocafort

If you're up for a raunchy night out – or a raunchy end to your evening – stop off here. With everything you could wish for in a naughty niterie, and recently relocated so about as clean and smart as it's ever going to be, XT is exactly what you'd expect from this saucy city. And more.

CAFÉ DE L'OPERA

- ℹ️ La Rambla 74
- ☎️ 93 302 41 80 🌙 Mon–Fri 8.30am– 2am; Sat–Sun 8.30am–3am Ⓜ️ Metro: Liceu

A mixed straight/gay (in that order) coffee shop with a long history as a hangout for post-performance opera queens. By day, it does great tapas, though it's best to skip the seats on the street and the upstairs overspill, and claim a doorway table instead (great for people-watching on the Rambla).

DANZATORIA

ℹ️ A. Tibidabo 61
📞 93 211 62 61
www.danzatoria-barcelona.com
🕒 Tues–Sat 9pm–2.30am
Ⓜ️ Metro: Tibidabo

The latest thing: a dance bar set in the grounds of a mansion house on Tibidabo, with an enormous dance area in the backyard. Mixed straight/gay, unlike its white-trash sister club in Port Olímpic, but very gay at weekends.

SWEET

ℹ️ C. Casanova 75
🕒 Tues–Thur 8pm–2.30am; Fri–Sat 8pm–3am Ⓜ️ Universitat

Much calmer than your average gay bar, this is somewhere to regain your buzz, get in a couple of quiet drinks and recharge for your next assault.

LA LUNA

ℹ️ Diagonal 323
🕒 Mon 5pm–8.30am; Thur–Fri 5pm–8.30am, 11pm–3am, 5pm–10.30am
Ⓜ️ Metro: Verdaguer

If it's one of those nights when you just can't seem to go home, you'll probably find yourself at some point at this most famous of After Hours up on Diagonal. The music segues from club hits to oldies and you'll find the crowd very welcoming. No matter what state you're in.

EAGLE

ℹ️ Passeig de San Joan, 152 📞 93 207 56 58
www.eaglespain.com
🕒 Fri–Sat 10pm–3am; Sun–Thur 10pm–2.30am
Ⓜ️ Metro: Verdaguer

Where Bearsalona comes to play. A dress-code bear pit for guys into jeans, leather, rubber, uniform and the rougher side of life. There's a busy dark-room and occasional theme nights, including underwear-only sessions.

FREE WOMEN

ℹ️ C. Casanova 43
🔇 No phone
🕒 Sun–Thur 4pm–1am; Fri–Sat 4pm–2am
Ⓜ️ Metro: Urgell

A cosy lesbian café serving drinks in a laid-back gallery space.

NEW CHAPS

ℹ️ A. Diagonal, 365
📞 93 215 53 65
🕒 Mon–Thur 9pm–3am; Fri–Sat 9pm– 3.30am; Sun 7pm–3am

A meeting place and playpen for guys into leather and denim. There's a busy labyrinth and dark room. On Sunday

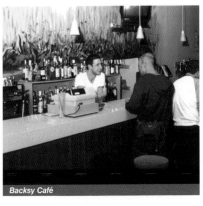

Backsy Café

OUT ON THE TOWN

Wilkommen to Café Dietrich

afternoon there's also a happy hour, with two for one drinks.

OUI CAFÉ

ℹ️ C. Consell de Cent 247
📞 93 451 45 70 🕐 Sun–Thur 5pm–2am; Fri–Sat 5pm–3am 🚇 Metro: Universitat

Popular meeting place with lots of cosy crannies, especially popular with guys who don't look old enough to drink. Serving coffee and cocktails from early evening, with a neat outdoor terrace in summer. The staff could show more interest in customers other than their regulars, though.

LA PEDRERA DE NIT

ℹ️ C. Provença 261
📞 93 484 59 95
www.funcaixacat.com
🚇 Diagonal 💶 €10

The unparalleled rooftop bar at Gaudí's La Pedrera is a dressy hangout in the summer months. Not gay, but popular with gay locals

and tourists alike. Beware the steep entry fee.

LA ROSA

ℹ️ C. Brusi 39, Plaça Molina 📞 93 474 61 66
🕐 Thur–Sun 10pm–3am
🚇 Metro: Fontana

The first ever lesbian bar to open in Barcelona, in the Sant Gervasi district, is now an older women's haunt. It remains a welcoming, neighbourhood bolthole, if a little out of the way, with gentle music and a genteel, discerning clientele. Great for surreptitious hand-holding over a glass of wine.

SCHILLING

ℹ️ C. Ferran 23
📞 93 317 67 87
🕐 Mon–Sat 10am–2.30am; Sun noon–2.00am 🚇 Liceu

Mock Viennese coffee bar popular during the day with intellectual homos, and with barflies at night. Noisy and smoky.

SOUVENIRS

ℹ️ C. Noi del Sucre 75, Viladecans (outside Barcelona), A-16 motorway (exit 50)
🌐 www.matineegroup.com
🕐 Sat, Sun, and before festival days, from 1am
🚇 No metro; RENFE train to Viladecans

One of Barcelona's best after-hours gay club that's not even in Barcelona! A motorway-side warehouse serving up banging house to a wasted crowd.

LA TERRAZA CLUB

ℹ️ A. Marques de Comillas, Poble Espanyol
📞 93 423 12 85
www.nightsungroup.com
🕐 Thur–Sun (May–Oct only) midnight–6am
🚇 Metro: Espanya

As the name suggests, it's a large open-air club on a palm tree-lined terrace in the Poble Espanyol (see pp. 49–50) serving up house to a mixed, up for it, posey crowd. Drag shows at weekends, when it's gayest. A real Barcelona experience, and one of the best and biggest clubs in town, so it's worth going once just to say you've been. Summer months only.

Barcelona/Sitges events

Not sure when's the best time to visit Barcelona and Sitges? The place goes a shade pinker than usual three times a year. First, during the Sitges Mardi Gras, a traditional and wild street carnival held in the seaside town every February in which gay locals play a visible part. Then, if you're lucky and Barcelona's gay burghers have got their act together, there's a national Pride event at the end of June (though it supposedly alternates with Madrid). Check if it's going ahead, and in which city, in the news section of the www.gay.es website, or in the local gay press. More dependable is the annual International Lesbian and Gay Film Festival, an established calendar highlight held in Barcelona every October/early November. Check www.festivalbarcelona.com for details. And remember to book accommodation in advance, as demand is even higher during such events.

A night out

Cinematic wonder

Playing Around Town

Barcelona's performance art scene is as varied as the stars it has brought to the international stage: from opera legends José (Josep in Catalan) Carreras and Montserrat Caballé, who occasionally perform at the splendidly renovated Liceu theatre, to its sparkiest theatrical troupe, Els Joglars.

When it comes to cinema, Barcelonans are fanatics, and the city has everything from local fleapits to state-of-the-art multiplexes, as well as an IMAX in the port. Wherever you go, tickets generally are cheaper on *el dia del espectador*, usually Mondays and Wednesdays, and often for the first showing of the day.

Tickets for most performance events are available from the ServiCaixa hotline (902 33 22 11). For detailed listings, newsstands sell the weekly *Guía del Ocio*, or check out the comprehensive Exit section of the daily *El Periódico*.

But if it's free street theatre you're after, every Sunday morning outside the La Seu cathedral in the Barri Gòtic, ageing locals put on a display of Catalonia's unintentionally hilarious national dance, the *sardana*.

OUTLINES

GRAN TEATRE DEL LICEU

🛈 La Rambla 51–9

📞 93 485 99 13 (ServiCaixa)

www.liceubarcelona.com

Ⓜ Metro: Liceu. Bus: 14, 38, 59

One of the greatest opera houses in Europe and now one of its most technologically advanced, the Liceu has twice been rebuilt after major fires, reopening in 1999 after its most recent misfortune. Tickets for the star-studded performances are hard to come by. But the schedule is dotted with semi-staged performances and recitals of interesting lesser works, often by Catalan composers, which are sometimes easier to attend.

IMAX in the port

TEATRE NACIONAL DE CATALUNYA

🛈 Plaça de les Arts 13
🌐 93 306 57 00
www.teatrelliure.com
Ⓜ Metro: Monumental, Glòries. Bus: 6, 7, 10, 56, 62

A grand public theatre inaugurated in 1997 to bring a spot of culture to the run-down Glòries area. A glass temple perched on a sweep of steps, it's as impressive outside as in, with two auditoriums in one complex. The programme runs the gamut from Greek tragedies to new Catalan commissions.

YELMO CINEPLEX

🛈 C. Salvador Espriu 61, Vila Olímpica
🌐 93 221 75 85
www.yelmocineplex.es
Ⓜ Metro: Ciutadella-Vila Olímpica

This unremarkable shopping mall complex deserves a mention for its late-night showings (*madrugadas*) on Fridays and Saturdays. With 15 films – mostly Hollywood blockbusters with Spanish subtitles – it is a haven for cinema buffs and insomniacs alike, and you can always go out clubbing afterwards or drink in the nearby marina. Be prompt because the screens sell out quickly.

IMAX PORT VELL

🛈 Moll d'Espanya
🌐 93 225 11 11
Ⓜ Metro: Barceloneta, Drassanes. Bus: 14, 36, 57, 59, 64, 157

A mix of Spanish, Catalan and English language giant-screen showings (some in 3D), including a couple of midnight sessions.

PALAU DE LA MÚSICA CATALUNYA

🛈 C. Sant Francesc de Paula 2 🌐 93 295 72 00
www.palaumusica.org
Ⓜ Metro: Urquinaona. Bus: 17, 19, 40, 45

A remarkable Modernista building that hosts the most prestigious events in the city's classical music calendar. Highlights include an annual guitar festival, and every 26 December, *Sant Esteve,* a showpiece classical concert that's a sellout and broadcast live on Catalan tele-vision. The acoustics are notoriously bad, sacrificed on the altar of Modernista aesthetics. Take in the latter on a pre-concert guided tour and check out the restaurant in the new extension, open from 10am–3.30pm.

CINES ARENAS

🛈 C. Tarragona 5–7
🌐 93 423 11 69
🕐 Daily from 4pm
Ⓜ Metro: Espanya

Tucked behind Hotel Plaza, this low-key cinema plays arty Spanish and Latino movies with a gay flavour – like Ralf Koenig's interpretation of Lisístrata – and occasional racy Super 8 flicks in the main auditorium. If you can't follow the action, there are more hardcore goings on in the porno-bar.

MÉLIÈS CINEMES

🛈 C. Villaroel 102
🔗 93 451 00 51
☀ Tues–Sun 🔟 Metro: Urgell. Bus: 14, 20, 38, 59
🕼 €4.20; Mon €3

Cinephile heaven: a two-screen rep cinema showing *versió original* (original version) films,

mostly big-screen classics and arthouse staples with Catalan or Spanish subtitles. Regular double and triple bills keep the film buffs coming back.

INTERNATIONAL LESBIAN AND GAY FILM FESTIVAL

www.festivalbarcelona.com

The Festival Internacional de Cinema Gai i Lesbic is held in Barcelona every October in venues across the city, screening queer film from around the world. During the 10-day festival, bars

and clubs in the Gaixample throw lively party events.

FONT MÀGICA
See p.50.

PALAU SANT JORDI

🛈 A. de l'Estadí
🔗 93 481 11 92
🔟 Espanya, then escalators. Bus: 50

If it's live pop music you're after, all the big names like Madonna, Whitney and Pink have played this high-tech sports hall. In 2002 it hosted the MTV Europe Music Awards.

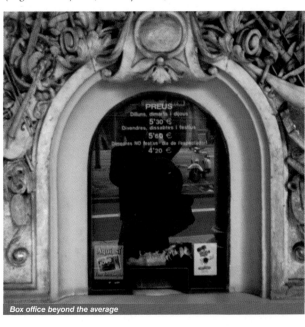

Box office beyond the average

Try pedal power . . .

Working Out

Got calories to burn? It's easy in Barcelona. New York-style gym chains have landed and locals are smitten. Gays and straights alike proudly carry their kit in the nifty string bags from DiR fitness clubs. If treadmills aren't your thing, join the rollerbladers along Platje de la Barceloneta, try your hand (and upper arms) at La Foixarda, an urban climbing wall up on Montjuïc, or go sailing from the Base Nàutica (93 221 04 32, www.basenautica.net) that marks the start of the gay beach, Mar Bella. Alternatively, you can hire a bike (see p.96), or take a two-wheeled guided tour of the city. Packages are offered by Mike's Bike Tours (93 301 36 12, www.mikesbiketours.com) and Biketours by Biciclot (93 307 74 75, www.biciclot.net). Runners can happily train along the relatively flat seafront, or, for tougher terrain, on Montjuïc or Collserola, the hill opposite. Both tough inclines are included on the route of the Marathon Catalunya, held in Barcelona every March (www.redestb.es/marathon_cat).

OUTLINES

EUROPOLIS

ⓘ Travessera de les Corts 252–254

☎ 93 363 29 92
www.europolis.es

🕙 Mon–Fri 7am–11pm; Sat 8am–8pm; Sun 9am–3pm

🚍 Hospital Clinic. Bus: 14, 31, 38, 54, 59, 63, 66

💰 €9.50 a day for non-members

In the Gaixample, so you know you're going to find some of the boys a-pumpin', this fresh new sports facility is actually run by Holmes Place, the UK gym chain, so you know it's going to be swish. There's a massive area for pounding treadmill, a pleasant indoor pool as well as organised exercise classes (a great place to meet men in tight clothing) such as Spinning, Aquaerobics, Pump and Step. It's a Catalan joint but with the Holmes Place connection, there'll be English speakers.

Relaxation time

Well-equipped gym

DIR EIXAMPLE

ℹ️ Passatge Domingo 6–8
📞 93 450 48 18. General
DiR info: 901 30 40 30
www.dirfitness.es
🕐 Daily 7am–11pm
Ⓜ️ Metro: Passeig de
Gràcia. Bus: 24, 43, 44, 54,
64, 66, 67, 68
💳 Rates on request

Not gay but a popular Barcelona-wide chain with the set who like to sweat in style. This branch on the edge of the Gaixample has a large work-out room, massage rooms, steam bath and walk-in solariums, plus more than 80 classes from aerobics to cardio kickboxing.

LA FITNESS

ℹ️ Bruc 122
📞 93 208 22 00
www.lafitness.co.uk
Ⓜ️ Metro: Diagonal,
Passeig de Gràcia,
Verdaguer. Bus: 6, 15, 20,
33, 34, 43, 44, 45, 47
💳 Day membership €12.
Other rates on request

The British chain recently opened in Barcelona, mostly attracting a business crowd. Popular with guests from the nearby Hostal Qué Tal (see p.123).

AL PUNT DE TROBADA

ℹ️ C. Badajoz 24
📞 93 225 05 95
bicipuntrobada@hotmail.com
🕐 April–Sept, daily
9am–3pm, 5pm–9pm;
Oct–Mar, Mon–Sat
9am–2pm, 4pm–8pm, Sun
9am–5pm. Ⓜ️ Metro:
Llacuna. Bus: 32, 92
💳 AmEx, MasterCard,
Visa

Bike hire shop with friendly, knowledgeable staff, perfectly placed in the Poble Nou district for a spot of cycling along the seafront.

Mountain bikes and rollerblades from €3.60/hour, €10.80/half day, €16/day. Tandems also available.

PISCINES BERNAT PICORNELL

ⓘ A. de l'Estadi 30–40, Montjuïc

🅰 93 423 40 41
www.picornell.com

🕑 Mon–Fri 7am–midnight, Sat 7am–9pm, Sun 7.30am–8pm (Oct–May, Sun 7.30am–4pm)

🅜 Metro: Espanya, then escalators; Paral.lel then funicular. Bus: 50, 61 Bus Turístic

🅥 €8 (€4.50 June–Sept). Cash only

Built for the 1970 European swimming championships and dolled up for the Olympics, Montjuïc's impressive twin pools (the outdoor pool is heated in winter) are easily the best place to do laps in the city. Consider the 20-minute walk up the hill from Espanya metro station as your warm-up. The indoor pool hosts nude sessions after hours on Saturday nights and Sunday afternoons (call for more details) and there's a weights room attracting a fair proportion of gay men and lesbians.

Staff speak little English but are friendly.

SAUNA GALILEA

ⓘ Calàbria 59

🅰 93 426 79 05

🕑 Mon–Thur noon–midnight, then 24hrs; Fri noon–Sun midnight

🅜 Metro: Rocafort, Poble Sec 🅥 €11

Not far from the Gaixample, Galilea attracts a mix of ages and sizes with its clean sauna and steam rooms split over four floors. The five-man Jacuzzi on the top floor is a popular secluded spot. The myriad private cabins have videos on loop. Busiest days are cut-price Tuesdays and Thursdays, when it's full of students. Weekend mornings 6–9am, entry is reduced and includes free breakfast.

SAUNA CASANOVA

ⓘ C. Casanova 57

🅰 93 323 78 60

🕑 Daily 24hrs

🅜 Metro: Hospital Clinic, Urgell

🅥 €12.50

Barcelona's busiest sauna is an acquired taste. The dirty perspex water chute that decorates the entrance stairwell isn't the most pleasant welcome, but once inside it's a clean enough place. Towels and slippers are included in the price and the door staff are friendly and speak good English, but the clientele are notoriously sniffy. Busy yourself in the darkened sauna and steam rooms, or watch TV and chat in the chill-out lounge.

Casanova, cleaner on the inside

Sant Bartomeu i Tecla on the Sitges skyline

Sitges

A guide within a guide

Stepping Out

A 20-minute train ride from Barcelona's Sants station, down the Costa Garraf, is the historic seaside resort of Sitges (pronounced Seet-yes). Its narrow cobbled streets, beautiful buildings, 7 kilometres of wide Mediterranean beaches (17 in total) and shallow shoreline – oh, and same-sex couples from all over the world holding hands without a care – make Sitges a must–do for any visitor to Barcelona.

A popular retreat and party town for avant-garde artists in the late 19th century (Picasso and his set chilled out here), the town retains a cultured sparkle, even though its palette is decidedly rainbow-coloured these days. In summer there's even a special 'pink night-train' that shuttles tired revellers back to Barcelona during the small hours. Ask at the station or tourist information office on C. Sínia Morera (93 894 42 51, www.sitges.org).

My Top Sights

Església de Sant Bartomeu i Tecla

ⓘ Plaça de la Església
◉ Open only during Mass: Mon–Fri at 7.30pm, Sat 8pm, Sun 9am–noon

The most iconic landmark in Sitges, this 17th-century church dominates the skyline, staring out over the Mediterranean from its promontory. The original steps leading up to the church were eroded by the sea, though the church itself remains defiant against the elements. Local legend has it that fishermen's wives used to climb the bell tower to watch out for their returning spouses. Perhaps from here you can pick

out yours along the 4 kilometres of beachfront to the east. While its location
and views are more arresting than its interior, the impressive Baroque organ
has its admirers. The church becomes a focal point during the town's
Festa Major celebrations in August, in which locals parade *gegants*
(giant puppets) through the streets before a superb firework display.

Museu Maricel

🛈 C. Follonar 🌞 Summer: Tues–Sun 10am–2pm, 5pm–9pm. Rest of year: Tues–Fri
10am–1.30pm, 3pm–6.30pm, Sat 10am–7pm, Sun 10am–3pm
💰 €3 (or entry to all three Sitges museums, €5.45). Free first Wed of the month

Just beyond the church, the Palau Maricel was commissioned by an
American millionaire and Sitges devotee Charles Deering to house his art
collection from medieval times – including Romanesque wall paintings and
altarpieces – to Renaissance woodcarvings and 20th-century works.
Constructed by Miquel Utrillo, the palace (once a hospital) is ornately tiled
and has several magnificent terraces. The mirador, considered by many as the
highlight of the museum, offers a breathtaking sea view and explains why
the palace is named after sea and sky (*mar i cel*). From June to September, it
hosts popular midweek summer night concerts.

A Marques de Montroig

Sitges's gayest drag – which isn't saying much – this café-lined strip
leading to the beach becomes a catwalk by day, colonised by gay boys
and girls sipping *café con leche* while eyeing up the passing talent through
dark glasses. Everyone seems to decamp here for the siesta – great for
people-spotting. If this is café central, then C. de 1er de Maig, the street
it feeds into across the Plaça de la Industria, is gay clubland. With its
banging gay clubs, it is better known locally, albeit ever so respectfully, as
Sin Street. To swap admiring glances in the afternoon, pitch up early at
the Café de Montroig whose terrace offers the most eye-catching
vantage point.

Platja de la Bassa Rodona

Though the entire Sitges beachfront is friendly, tolerant, and mixed, the
stretch in front of the Calípolis Hotel is the biggest gay draw; you'll find the
highest density of stripped-down gay men and lesbians here during the
day. The gazing at toned and tanned bodies is unsubtle, and the
atmosphere friendly and social rather than intimidating. A 10-minute
stroll along the beach from Sant Bartomeu church, it's where everyone
gathers in high season to dissect the adventures of the previous night; if
you made an impression on the scene, expect tongues to be wagging as
you rub in your sun lotion. There are sun loungers for hire and showers

for getting the sand out of those awkward places. Look out for the families of friendly wild cats miaowing around the piers.

Platja del Home Mort

Sitges's delightfully named gay nudist area – Playa del Muerto in Spanish, or Dead Man's Beach – is a hike and a half, pitched some 4 kilometres from the main gay beach, and involves an element of orienteering. Wear sensible shoes and be prepared for an hour's power-walking.

Walk the length of the Passeig Marítim seafront to the Hotel Terramar (or catch the Bus Urbà from the station, which terminates here). Continue along the rocky beach if the tide is out, or follow the road to L'Atlàntida Disco; a cab from the town centre to this, the last reachable point by transport, costs €10 or less. Now climb the hill path and walk along the railway. Stay on the sea side of the railway for the path to the beach, or cross over to the woods to join the other gay men resting in the shade.

The first beach is the mixed nudist beach; keep going for another 10 minutes to Platja del Home Mort which is almost exclusively for gay men. In high season, a shack serves expensive cold drinks and snacks – as this is quite a trek, it's a captive market. The beach is pebbly, so rent a lounger or bring a big towel.

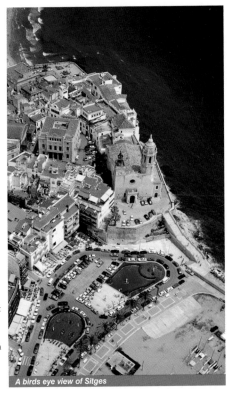

Now, there is an easier way to sunbathe nude in Sitges. There are a couple of designated beaches to the left of Sant Bartomeu church, but naked bodies here tend to attract stares from tourists at the Mirador. Might be worth an hour's walk to Platja del Home Mort, after all…

A birds eye view of Sitges

Sitges

Sitges: Around Town

A DAY OUT

There are few must-sees in Sitges. But thanks to strict planning regulations, the narrow, twisted streets of the Old Town remain timewarped, with rows of whitewashed matchbox-style houses and pretty plaças. Simply walking around is to be immersed in traditional Catalan character.

Those coming to Sitges for the buzz and the beachlife will want to stake their place on the sand as soon as possible. They should follow the crowds streaming off the *rodalies* (local train) from Barcelona – its streets are so tight, and the ride so easy, you'll be glad you left the hire car behind (see box p.104) – along all routes downhill to the Passeig Marítim. As you pass, make a mental note of Carrers Espalter, Bonaventura and Bonaire; with their numerous gay clubs and bars, these are the backbone of the gay scene.

Those here for a bit of sightseeing rather than just copious sun should head from the station along C. Artur Carbonell to pick up the local gay listings guides and maps at the Hotel Liberty. (See p.126.) Take a left into Sant Francesc, and you'll arrive at Plaça Cap de la Vila, the small main square – so small there's barely room for a Smart car to swing around it.

From here, those interested in the Museu Romàntic – which lays bare the life of a wealthy 19th-century family in Sitges in a series of recreated period rooms – can head up C. Sant Francesc. Otherwise, it's on to C. Major, Sitges's shopping high street with its chic boutiques and not excessively tacky souvenir shops.

This leads us to Plaça del Ajuntament, whose neighbouring alleys house the town's two other collections, the Museu Cap Ferrat and Museu Maricel. But the crowning glory of this neighbourhood – literally – is the towering Església de Sant Bartomeu i Tecla in Plaça de la Església (see pp.99–100). Come back to experience Mass – all day Sundays – and get access to the rooftop for fantastic views.

Now it's time to hit the beach. Platja de la Fragata and Platja de la Ribera both have volleyball nets. But for somewhere to catch the sun and be seen rather than exert yourself, walk along the wide seafront, Passeig de la Ribera, to the gay beach, Platja de la Bassa Rodona (see pp.100–101). To lose the crowds, head further down the snaking beachfront. There's a gay nudist beach about an hour's trek from here. (see p.101).

When you've had your fill of the sun, head up C. 1er de Maig, which is referred to inexplicably as Dos de Maig and feeds into C. Marqués de

Montroig, the drag of gay cafés that's packed with life all summer. Pull up a seat (again, space permitting) or just lean with a bottle of Dos Equis and start posing. Only a matter of hours till the clubs open…

Hit the beaches for a game of volleyball

GETTING TO AND AROUND SITGES

To get to Sitges, take the **train** from Barcelona-Sants station. A single ticket is €2.40 and trains leave every 20 minutes, usually from platforms 5 and 6 (look for trains to Vilanova). The journey takes between 20 and 30 minutes, depending on stops.

With its narrow streets and tight corners, Sitges is particularly vehicle-unfriendly – here, the pedestrian is king. The C-31 route from Barcelona also tends to be congested (the expensive toll route, C-32, less so). Ever get the impression that the Catalans want you to use public transport?

A good way to do the seafront is on two wheels. **Cycles** are for hire from €9 a day at La Bicicleta (Centre Comercial Oasis, tel 93 894 87 58). The terminally lazy can call a **taxi** in Sitges on 93 894 35 94 or 93 894 13 29.

OUTLINES

MUSEU ROMÀNTIC

ⓘ C. Sant Gaudenci 1 📞 93 894 29 69
🕓 Mid June–mid Sept,Tues–Sun
10am–9pm; mid Sept–mid June Tues–Fri
9.30am–2pm, 4pm–6pm; Sat 9.30am–
2pm, 4pm–8pm; Sun 9.30am–2pm
Ⓝ €3 (or entry to all three Sitges
museums, €5.45)

See how aristocratic Catalans lived
at the end of the 19th century, at
the height of the *Renaixença*
(Renaissance), with a peek inside
this purposefully preserved family
home. Guided tours, offered every
hour, reveal a grand
Mediterranean house that was
built with rich architectural
flourishes – there's an impressive
main stairwell – that's decorated
rather more modestly by its less
extravagant former residents.

MUSEU CAP FERRAT

ⓘ C. Follonar
📞 93 894 03 64

🕓 Mid June–mid Sept Tues–Sun
10am– 9pm; mid Sept–mid June Tues–Fri
9.30am– 2pm, 4pm–6pm; Sat 9.30am–
2pm, 4pm–8pm; Sun 9.30am–2pm
Ⓝ €3 (or entry to all three Sitges
museums, €5.45)

Art buffs can shade from the sun
in this former home and art
studio of Santiago Rusiñol, a
leading light of Modernisme who
counted Picasso and Miró among
his friends (they came to Sitges to
summer at his house). The
museum houses his impressive
collection of paintings and
drawings bequeathed on his death
to the town, including his own,
along with major works by
Picasso and El Greco.

MUSEU MARICEL
See p.100.

ESGLÉSIA DE SANT
BARTOMEU I TECLA
See p.99.

Out to Lunch

You'll be hard-pushed to eat cheaply in Sitges –
and in the summer, even the handful of bad
restaurants are full. Those on a tight budget
should avoid the seafront, where the hotels serve
hit-and-miss paella and pasta meals to the
Eurotrash crowd. For a Catalan *menú del dia*
around the €7 mark – probably the best deal in
town – try the relaxed **El Celler Vell** in the
heart of gayland. The **Sucré Salé** crêperie also
does good-value three-course lunch options or
try **Villa Lola**, a quaint juice and coffee bar
tucked around a bend near the Platja de la
Ribera beachfront.

EL CELLER VELL
ⓘ C. Sant
Bonaventura 21
📞 93 811 19 61
🍴 🍷

SUCRÉ SALÉ
ⓘ C. Sant Pau 39
📞 93 894 23 02
🍴 🍷

VILLA LOLA
ⓘ Passeig de la
Ribera
📞 No Phone
🍴 🍷

Sitges: Eating Out

If your wallet can stretch to it, it's relatively easy to eat well in Sitges. The Old Town is chock full of restaurants – C. de Sant Pau has a particularly strong concentration – and in high season it's worth dropping into one that takes your fancy on your way to the beach to guarantee a table later in the day. Fish and seafood are, inevitably for a fishing town, dishes of the day, but there are plenty of interesting international cuisine and vegetarian options to be had, too.

Cream of the Cuisine

Ma Maison

ℹ C. Bonaire 28
☎ 93 894 60 54 🍴 🍴

A gay-run garden restaurant in the heart of gaytown that scores full marks for ambience alone. The setting is idyllic – a tree-lined courtyard with plenty of leafy boughs, it's the perfect spot for a long, lazy lunch in the shade during a scorching summer afternoon. There's a select number of tables, mostly set for four, but romantic couples can be accommodated somewhere more snug. That it's impossibly pretty doesn't distract from the quality of the French-influenced modern European menu, which is impeccable. Deservingly, a much-loved gay fixture, popular with men and women.

> **The following price guides have been used for eating out and indicate the price for a main course:**
>
> 🍴 = **cheap** = under €8
>
> 🍴 = **moderate** = €8–€17
>
> 🍴 = **expensive** = €17+

Can Pagès

ℹ C. Sant Pere 24–26
📞 93 894 11 95

One of the favourite eating options in Sitges has a renowned dynasty of chefs behind it. The Ramos family have long been offering typical Catalan seaside fare in rhyme with the season. Set back from the seafront, the interior is rustic in style, and there's a popular terrace that opens for the hot summer months. Fish fans will be happy with the inventive seafood stews, while there's a greater emphasis than most other restaurants in town on red meat, too. It's got that particular market cornered – the barbecue grill is the stuff of local legend.

Al Fresco

ℹ C. Pau Barrabeitg 4
📞 93 894 06 00

Foodies rate this among the best restaurants Sitges has to offer – and its menu is by no stretch typical of the town. Though there are regional influences (especially on the fish side), the menu is a globetrotting affair, borrowing heavily from the Middle East and the Pacific Rim as much as around the Mediterranean coast. This arty, off-the-wall backstreet bistro is the only place in town serving kangaroo.

Seafood snack in Sitges

SUCRÉ SALÉ
ℹ C. Sant Pau 39
📞 93 894 23 02

Busy garden restaurant with a menu of 'crêpes and things' that's light and varied. Besides the inventive pancake menu (not an especially Catalan speciality, but it keeps north Europeans happy), there are salads and chilled soups – perfect for the summer palate, and plenty for the healthy eater, too. All served in a delightful outdoor setting, or romantically low-lit indoors.

PIC NIC
ℹ Paseo de la Ribera
📞 93 811 00 40
www.matasarnalot.com

You're not going to come here for dinner but if you're stretched out on that gay beach you're at least going to slip in here to use their toilets. Nice and basic with a terrace overlooking the Speedos, it's great for a lunchtime salad and bocadillo de tortilla francesa and a jug of sangria. They do nice icecreams too!

Best of the Rest

MONTY'S
ⓘ Passeig de la Ribera

Great little Italian with cheapo pasta dishes and top-notch vegetarian options – perhaps the largest selection in town. Inevitably perhaps, it's very popular with lesbians.

GABRIEL
ⓘ C. Sant Gaudenci 9
☎ 93 894 30 46

Intimate, gay-run French bistro – the calling card features a skin-headed sailor wielding his catch of the day. There's à la carte, but also a dinner buffet worth picking over.

BEACH HOUSE
ⓘ San Pau, 34
☎ 93 894 90 29
www.beachhouse
sitges.com

You've got to love the Aussies that have turned this whatever little place into a jumping hotspot (they only do it 'cause they get to spend five months of the year travelling the world). They're both gay, both top chefs and have cooked up a great atmosphere and

a super set menu for less than €20. And they're both cracking looking.

LA SANTA MARÍA
ⓘ Passeig Maritim 52
☎ 93 894 09 99
www.lasantamaria.com

Occupying the most privileged location on the beachfront, this hotel-restaurant's terrace is one of the most elegant spots in town to be served *paellas* and *mariscos*. The faded glamour about the place – down to the retro plasticky menus – appears to appeal to the upmarket international clientele who've come fresh from the beach.

EL XALET
ⓘ C. Illa de Cuba 35
☎ 93 811 00 70
www.elxalet.com

Fine dining in the luxuriant gardens of a perfectly preserved Modernista house with tables set up – here's the twist – next to an inviting swimming pool. Expect a warm welcome from the owners, a relaxed atmosphere, and a good-value set menu.

Sitges: Out on the Town

Sitges has been a gay magnet since the 1960s, when it first began pulling in Spain's same-sex artist couples who were drawn to it by its historical links with the avant-garde and alternative lifestyles. Today, it vies with Ibiza for the title of Europe's most popular homo resort. While smaller – its 20,000 population swells to 80,000 in summer, thanks largely to an influx of gays – it is considerably more cosmopolitan than its brasher Balearic rival.

Its growing reputation in gay circles has happily resulted in a significant leap in the number of gay women visitors in recent years. Fittingly, there are whispers of a substantial slew of planned lesbian venues – at the moment, women have 'invited guest' status in many of the men's bars. Ask around for details of new openings. If the tourist information office is clueless, the staff at Hotel Liberty – which hosts its own lesbian Sunday nighter which is open to the public – will sort you out. At the height of the season, chances are you'll be turned away from a club or two. But don't worry – and don't try phoning ahead to check, there's no point. Just head around the corner to the next.

My Top Clubs

Trailer

C. Angel Vidal 36   Daily midnight–6am www.trailerdisco.com

The legendary gay venue – celebrating 25 glorious years – that's always packed with hot and sweaty bodies dancing well into the morning.

Famed for its raucous Wednesday and Sunday night foam parties, plenty of revellers have reported difficulty getting the, er, watermarks out of their clubbing gear. Better check your clothes in, strip down to your under- or swimwear and get slippy with all the boys. Drinks are more pricey than at other venues, but you're guaranteed a night you won't forget.

Mediterraneo

ⓘ C. Sant Bonaventura 6
🕐 Daily 10pm–3.30am

One of the most popular and relaxed places for a boogie, this is where most of Sitges ends up after a night's boozing. The club doesn't get busy until about 1am, when it fills to the brim. It looks small from the outside but it's split over two floors, with a pleasant chill-out gallery decorated with real palm trees – cool! Musically, expect an unpretentious, pumping mix of the latest handbag dance sounds – hands-aloft diva vocal tracks in both English and Spanish rule the roost here.

Parrot's Pub

ⓘ Plaça de l'Industria 2
🕐 Daily from 5pm

The terrace opens early to catch the crowds coming in from the beach, and is a good place for early evening cocktails. Friendly and welcoming, Parrot's is popular with a relaxed mix of gay men, lesbians and their mates – basically, anyone who's under starter's orders

XXL

ⓘ C. Joan Tarrida 7
🕐 Daily 11pm–3.30am

One of the few places that stays open all year around, XXL is a well-established bar-cum-club that caters for all shapes and sizes – even regular, trim guys. The difference is that the music – and the scene – is heavier than most. Go for a spin around on the dance floor, or get drawn in by the X-rated vids playing all about the place. On Tuesday nights, it's time to strip off for the underwear parties. XXL is unpretentious fun, with friendly bar staff who go out of their way to make single travellers feel welcome. Not that you'll be single here for long.

So much to do

Who's a pretty boy?

for a night out in town. It's an unwritten local bylaw that the first drink of the night has to be in Parrot's. It's also worth popping in to pick up a copy of the free Sitges gay map and local listings rags. Essential.

Maripili

🛈 C. Joan Tarrida 14
⏰ Daily noon–3am

This is the centre of the women's scene in Sitges – the sole women-only joint. A friendly terrace café by day, it opens at midday and soon fills with chilled-out dykes from all over the world chatting about the previous night's conquests, while banishing hangovers with generous portions of hearty finger food. Once the sun's going down, and you've downed too much cappuccino and have watched the world go by (back to their hotels to tidy themselves up for another night out), the vibe shifts up a gear, becoming pre-clubby. It's worth popping back to pick up a flyer or two for the lesbian-approved gay clubs – and to check who's expected to show their face on the scene that night…

Best of the Rest

SEVEN

ℹ️ C. Nou 5

🕐 Daily 10pm–3am

A buzzing bar, popular with early worms as well as the various local ex-pats who prop it up until the cavalry arrive later. *El siete* is one of the first to get busy – and when it does, you can't move. Enjoy a pre-dinner cocktail and watch the crowds pour in.

BAR AZUL

ℹ️ Bonaventura 10

🕐 Daily 9pm–3am

This cabaret bar is not blue, as the name suggests, but bright orange. The name might have more to do with the blue movies it shows, as the sound system disconcertingly plays songs from the shows. There's a happy hour from 10pm to midnight in the summer months (April–October).

EL HORNO

ℹ️ C. Joan Tarrida 6

📞 93 894 09 09

🕐 Daily 5.30pm–3.30am

Just round the corner from Parrot's, and popular with the leather and denim crowd. Has a video room and backroom upstairs that hosts underwear parties on Tuesdays and Thursdays. Happy hour until 7pm.

THE B-SIDE BAR

ℹ️ C. Sant Gaudeneci 7

🕐 Daily 6pm–3am

Men-only bar, with darkroom and videos. Open all year round (closed Mondays October–June).

OREK'S BAR MUSICAL

ℹ️ Bonaire, 13

Come for the music or the backroom or the dirty videos but come with fun in mind, especially if there's a stripper shaking it about as there tends to be when the Golden Boys are in town. And look out for one of their 80s nights.

BOURBON'S

ℹ️ C. San Buenaventura 13

📞 93 894 33 47

🕐 Daily 10.30pm–3.30am

One for lovers of the

Organic club

Discothèque ad – Sitges style

dark – and a poseur's paradise. There are mirrors everywhere, even in the toilets, which reflect your full frontal around the gents. Get a few drinks down, then hit the dance floor or fumble your way around the darkroom until the lights come up.

EL CANDIL
ℹ C. Carreta 9
📞 93 894 78 36
🕐 Daily 10pm–3am

Familiar combination of dance floor, darkroom and video screens. A good mix of music keeps this bar busy and racked with talent.

BAR COMODIN
ℹ C. Tacó 5
📞 93 894 16 98
🕐 10pm–3am

Open every day except Tuesdays. Closed in November. As expected from the Tom of Finland flyers, you get an older crowd here. The Saturday-night drag shows are popular and worth the detour.

THE ORGANIC CLUB
ℹ C. Bonaire 15
📞 93 894 22 30
🕐 Daily 2am–6am

There's the latest sounds on a Friday and Saturday, and theme nights the rest of the week. Sunday's dance party is a step-back-in-time thrash with trash from the 70s onwards, and is always full with a lively, fun-loving crowd. On Tuesdays, Organic hosts a night at L'Alàntida, the open-air disco near the gay nudist beach. Check local press for details.

Surreal façade by Dalí

Out of Town

So you've partied in Barcelona and sunbathed in Sitges – what else does Catalunya offer the lesbian or gay traveller? Within a couple of hours of Barcelona there's Salvador Dalí's surrealist museum in Figueres; Cadaqués, the seaside village which inspired many of Picasso's greatest Cubist works; the mountain top monastery in Montserrat; the vineyard of Penedès… and even more sandy beaches by the bucket-load along the Costa Brava.The more adventurous might consider heading to Andorra, to the Pyrenees for skiing, to Valencia – or perhaps even to Ibiza, via the 9-hour ferry journey from the port (see pp.133–134).

Figueres

This windy inland town to the north of Barcelona was made famous by Salvador Dalí, who was born here in 1904 and died a recluse near the same spot in 1989. His museum is the main attraction, with exhibits as eyebrow-raising as the oddball's trademark pitchfork moustache.The surreal sights at the Teatre-Museu Dalí include a coin-operated Cadillac that rinses its interior with water; Dalí's rampart-like residence,Torre Galatea, topped with giant egg sculptures; and the Casa Mae West.The centrepiece is the artist's tomb, a wickedly macabre coffin fitted with a periscope that keeps watch over visitors. Figueres is also an increasingly popular base for a fabulous and mysterious lesbian community.You'll spot the ladies in wraparound sunglasses in the town's myriad cafés.

TEATRE-MUSEU DALÍ
🛈 Plaça Gala-Salvador Dalí 5 Figueres
📞 972 67 75 00
www.salvadordali.org
☀ July–Sept: daily 9am–7.45pm; Oct–June: daily 10.30am–5.45pm
💳 €10

OFICINA DE TURISME DE FIGUERES
🛈 Plaça del Sol   📞 972 50 31 55
🚗 By car: A7 or N11 to Figueres (120kms from Barcelona). By train: RENFE from Sants or Passeig de Gràcia (2 hrs), departures every hour. By bus: several departures daily with Barcelona Bus (93 232 04 59) from Estació del Nord (metro: Arc de Triomf). Journey time 2–3 hours

Montserrat

Overlooking the river Llobregat 50 kilometres northwest of Barcelona is Montserrat, the 'serrated mountain' made from pillars of ragged rock that's so unworldly its knife-edged form looks like giant sculpture rather than anything geological. The shadow cast by its tallest peak – some 1,236m high – is said to have influenced Gaudí's design for the Sagrada Família. Arrive by train at the nearby station and you can take a cable car to the Gothic monastery halfway up. Founded in 1025, its wooden statue of La Moreneta, the Black Virgin, inside the basilica has been the focus of Christian pilgrimages for centuries. Time a visit right and you'll catch a performance from the Escolanía, a boys' choir founded in the 13th century, one of Europe's oldest, which is rarely heard beyond the monastery walls (1pm and 7.10pm, Mon–Sat). While there are plenty of cliff walks to be enjoyed – and the sights across the valley are miraculous – mountain-climbing is also possible. Call the tourist office for more details.

MONESTIR DE MONTSERRAT
ⓘ Plaça de Santa Maria   Montserrat

OFICINA DE TURISME DE MONTSERRAT
ⓘ Plaça de la Creu   Montserrat
☎ 93 877 77 77
www.abadiamontserrat.net
🚗 By car: C58 to Montserrat exit, then 7km mountain road to monastery
By train: FGC train from Plaça d'Espanya

Montserrat monument

Glorious Girona

to Montserrat-Aeri station (up to 18 times daily), where you can get the cable car across.

 Ask for all-inclusive ticket

By bus: a Julià-Via bus leaves Sants bus station daily at 9am (earlier in summer), returning to Barcelona at 5pm. Journey time 75 mins.

Girona

Historically a tug-of-love between the Jews, Christians and Muslims, this well-preserved medieval hilltop town that is the largest in northern Catalunya is the undeniable jewel of the Costa Brava (not difficult, perhaps). At street level, it's a maze of steep stairs, narrow alleys and passageways worth exploring on foot. Must-sees include the colossal cathedral, a benchmark of Catalan Gothic that also has the world's largest nave (architects said it would never hold), 12th-century Arab baths *Banys Àrabs*, and the Pont de la Peixateries, an iron bridge built over the river Onyar by Eiffel (he of Parisian tower fame).

By car: A7 or N11 to Girona exit. 75kms
By train: RENFE from Sants or Passeig de Gràcia (1hr 15mins). Hourly 6am–9.15pm
By bus: Barcelona Bus, 3–7 daily, from Estació del Nord

OFICINA DE TURISME DE GIRONA
Rambla Llibertat 1
972 22 65 75

Tarragona

Declared a UNESCO World Heritage Site in 2000, this seaside city is one of Spain's oldest. It was the site of a military camp dating from the 3rd century BC that became the capital of Roman Iberia. Unsurprisingly, the sights within the old walled centre err on the imperial side: there's an ancient amphitheatre where many a gladiator met his end, and the remains of the vaulted circus (Circ Romà) once used for high-speed chariot racing. Thrillseekers today should head out of town to the new Universal Studios attraction, Port Aventura, for white-knuckle rides. There's also a magnificent Gothic cathedral, while nature lovers should not miss a boat trip around the wetlands of the nearby Ebre delta, which is a haven for 300 species of birds (and especially popular with flamingos).

AMFITEATRE ROMÀ
ⓘ Parc del Miracle 📞 977 24 25 79

CIRC ROMÀ
📞 977 24 19 52 🚇 Rambla Vella

PORT AVENTURA
ⓘ Apartado 90, Villa-Sec, Tarragona
📞 902 20 22 20 www.portaventura.es/
🕐 Open daily from 10am Mar–Nov
🎟 One-day pass: adults €37, children €30. Two-day pass: adults €53.50, children €43.

DELTA DE L'EBRE
📞 Information: 977 74 01 00
🚌 By car: A2, then either A7 via Vilafranca, or toll-free N340 (Molins de Rei exit). 100kms from Barcelona. By train: RENFE from Sants or Passeig de Gràcia. Hourly departures 6am–9.30pm. 1hr–1hr 30mins By bus: Nine buses from Barcelona Nord on weekdays, just two at weekends. Takes 1hr 30 mins

OFICINA DE TURISME DE TARRAGONA
ⓘ C. Fortuny 4 📞 977 23 34 15
www.tarragonaturisme.es

Cadaqués

Upmarket and a bolt hole for intellectuals, Cadaqués is to early 20th-century modern art what Giverny is to Impressionism. This whitewashed Costa Brava village with its bays, coves and isolated crags along the Cap de Creus peninsula moved Dalí (who had a house here) to speak of its 'grandiose geographic delirium' and entice his set, including Picasso, to paint here, too. See the fruits of their labours at the Museu de Cadaqués. Today, it retains its reputation as a suntrap for the rich holidaying Barcelona elite, and is perfect for wandering, for strolls along the pretty pebble beaches, and for eating in pricey but impeccable seafood restaurants.

MUSEU DE CADAQUÉS
ⓘ C. de Narcís Monturiol 📞 972 25 88 77
🚌 By car: A7 to exit 4, then C260 to Cadaqués (2hrs) By bus: between two and five SAFRA buses (972 25 87 13) leave Estacio del Nord every day; Barcelona buses offer two services a day. Journey times 2hrs 15 mins

OFICINA DE TURISME DE CADAQUÉS
ⓘ C. del Cotxe 2 📞 972 25 83 15

Cadaqués, whitewashed Costa Brava village

Vilafranca de Penedès

The Penedès brand is now a familiar sight in bottle shops around the world, with this increasingly regarded wine-growing region, whose monks have been producing since the 11th century, known especially for its Cava (sparkling Catalan white) (see p.77) and various robust reds – as well as the occasional cheeky riesling. Visitors are welcome at many of the sprawling vineyards in the area (it's so large you're better off exploring in a car), while the Gothic palace in the town of Vilafranca de Penedès houses the impressive Museu del Vi. The small entrance fee includes a tasting. The largest and most important winemaker in the area, Miguel Torres, offers free tours and tastings at his vineyard (by appointment only).

MUSEU DEL VI

ℹ️ Palau Reial 📞 93 890 05 82
🕐 Tues–Sat 10am–2pm, 4pm–7pm; Sundays and festival days 10am–2pm; closed Monday 🎟️ €3

TORRES VINEYARD

ℹ️ Fina El Maset, Pacs del Penedès
📞 93 817 74 87 www.torres.es
🕐 6am–10pm 🚗 By car: A2, then A7 to Vilafranca. 55kms from Barcelona
By train: RENFE to Vilafranca from Sants or Plaça Catalunya (45mins), departures every hour

OFICINA DE TURISME DE VILAFRANCA DE PENEDÈS

ℹ️ C. Cort 14 📞 93 892 03 58

Checking In

There's no such thing as low season in Barcelona – the city is always crammed with tourists. And at the height of summer, there's never quite enough accommodation to go round, hence the new arrivals snuggled up on the beach or checking into Sauna Casanova (see p.97) for the night. But if you book in advance, there are plenty of decent rooms going cheap.

Gay couples rarely confront problems in hotel receptions. But if you are booking into a straight hotel, before you arrive fax them you and your partner's names, confirming that you want a *cama doble* (double bed), just so there's no confusion.

At the lowest end of the market are the greatest bargains. And we're not talking flea-ridden backpackers' hostels, but *hostals*. A typically Spanish invention, *hostals* are usually clean, friendly and basically furnished townhouse apartments. Showers and bathrooms are often shared, though more upmarket operations will have en-suite options. They're a great way to keep costs down; get on with the owners and you've got a friend, tour guide and concierge to help with ticket bookings and restaurant recommendations. The downside is that they are often housed in old buildings, with thin walls and uncarpeted floors, so things can get noisy. Light sleepers might need a set of earplugs – but that's a small price to pay (cash only, of course).

Although it's worth having somewhere to stay in Barcelona before you arrive, those stuck for a place should make their first stop-off the tourist information centre on Plaça de Catalunya (see p.135), which, for a small fee, will find you a room from a daily updated list of available accommodation.

Hotel Arts Barcelona

ⓘ C. Marina 19–21 **⚡** 93 221 10 00   Fax 93 221 10 70
www.ritzcarlton.com/hotels/barcelona **Ⓜ** Ciutadella-Vila Olimpica **⬤** **③**

Barcelona's ritziest hotel is a landmark on its shoreline. At 44 storeys high, it is also the tallest building in Spain.

It's a popular choice with visiting dignitaries and celebrities – it was here that performers at the 2002 MTV Music Awards were put up in abject luxury – but it's also the perfect bolt hole for a gay stay.

Each of the luxurious rooms – 482 in total – has breathtaking panoramic views of the city and the sea, and it's a short walk from the Ramblas and the gay nudist beach Mar Bella. Great for a sightseeing city break or a dirty weekend.

The marble bathrooms have powerful walk-in power showers, there's a pillow menu and the offer of a butler-drawn bath. Before checking out, make sure you sweep up the freebie Bulgari toiletries. Pure indulgence!

Technophiles will love it, too. There's a Bang and Olufsen CD hifi, satellite TV and video in every room. When you've mastered those remote controls, there's always the electronically controlled blinds and light switches to play with...

As you'd expect, there's also an amazing gym – often seething with get-up-and-go execs – and a blissful beachfront pool for the less active.

If you've got the cash to splash, this is the place to stay.

Hotel Arts Barcelona – standing proud

The following price guides have been used for accommodation, per room per night

① = €10–€50
② = €50–€150
③ = over €150

Hotel Claris

ℹ Pau Claris 150 📞 93 487 62 62
Fax 93 215 79 70 www.slh.com/claris
Ⓜ Metro: Passeig de Gràcia

🛏 ③

Bang in the heart of the Eixample, this is one of the most style-conscious hotels in the city. Scoring high in the chi-chi stakes – it's a former 19th-century palace, renovated with glass and gold, and just off the designer shopping drag, Passeig de Gràcia – it's also a tantrum's throw from the gay bars of the Gaixample and the lesbian hangouts in Gràcia. Rooms are decked out in dark wood and plush drapes in a riot of bold, continental purples, reds and oranges (very Catalan). Each has its own entry salon, complete with TV and minibar. The bathrooms have a shell-shaped bath big enough for two.

It's the perfect hideout for homos from home.

Hostal Qué Tal

ℹ C. Mallorca 290 (corner with C. Bruc)
📞 93 459 23 66
www.quetalbarcelona.com
Ⓜ Metro: Passeig de Gràcia

🛏 ① Cash only

This long-standing favourite with gay travellers on tight budgets has a loyal following. Now it's so popular (admittedly, mostly with men, but women are made welcome) you have to book well in advance to secure a vacancy. And it's easy to see why. A converted Eixample townhouse with 14 rooms – and ever-expanding into neighbouring blocks – its rooms are clean, colourfully decorated in pastels, and deliciously cool in the sweaty summer months, when it's at its busiest.

Cheap and basic, Hostal Qué Tal (How Are You) has everything the low-rent traveller needs. Standard doubles come with a sink, wardrobe and a comfy bed, though there's also a choice of doubles with en-suite bathroom. A few rooms can sleep three and four persons – ideal for when sharing with friends. The shower rooms are kept immaculate by staff and guests alike. The prices speak for themselves, starting at €39 for a single with shared bath, €58 for a double with shared bath, and €74 for a double with own bath.

The staff are very friendly and discreet, speak first-rate English, and will happily keep you in mineral water and offer you freshly percolated coffee at any time of the day or night. They'll also advise you about where to go on the local scenes; the *hostal* is handy for both the gay and lesbian villages, pitched between the Gaixample and Gràcia. It's also within staggering distance from three of Barcelona's most popular men-only hangouts, New Chaps, Martins and the Eagle (so it gets the clone vote), as well as opposite Barcelona's hip LA Fitness gym. What more could you want?

Chill out

Hotel Axel

ⓘ Aribau 33 ☎ 93 323 93 93
www.hotelaxel.com
Ⓜ Metro: Universitat ◑ ②

Barcelona's hot gay hotel couldn't be better situated, slap bang in the middle of the Gaixample. Based in a huge 19th-century block, from the minute you step into the boutiquey lobby you know you're in for style, gay boys in Speedos and a great time. It may only have three stars but that's not reflected in the super-stylish all-white rooms with king-size beds and plasma screens (it's probably worth paying the extra for an 'exterior' room looking onto the street, while if you go for a Superior room, you get a pretty gallery with stained glass. There's a mini pool on the roof – perfect for showing off new swimwear or having a sunset cocktail – a Jacuzzi, library, gym… and lots of gay boys from all over the world cluttering up the place. And considering what they could probably get away with, the prices are sort of affordable. A new era in gay hotels has arrived!

Barcelona Rooms

ⓘ C. Comte d'Urgell 63
☎ 93 323 29 38, 629 159 759 (mob)
www.barcelonarooms.net
Ⓜ Metro: Urgell
◑ ①
Cash only

Barcelona Rooms is neither a hotel, a hostel, nor a *hostal*. Instead, it's a unique take on the guesthouse: gay-run, with 10 rooms done in modern décor, shared kitchen and TV lounge, and a convivial co-op feel.

There are his and hers shower rooms (it's as much for gay girls as for gay boys), a drinking fountain, and access to an iron (a rarity in most budget accommodation).

The shared kitchen is equipped with fridge, cooker, microwave and juicer – so you can shave costs off by self-catering. Though it's not a B&B, breakfast cereals are provided free. There's also a dining room for civilised 'house' get-togethers, which is also where newcomers are welcomed on their arrival with a glass of champagne.

Without doubt, this is the friendliest gay place to stay in Barcelona. Owners Pet and Sergi go out of their way to make all-comers welcome. They'll take you out for evening meals in the local tapas bar, and will happily escort you on a pub crawl until dawn, if so desired. And as if that wasn't enough, they'll also arrange massages for you with the live-in physiologist.

Located on a corner of the Gaixample, it's also handy for the airport: the A1 shuttle bus drops off and picks up right outside (ask the driver for Gran Via Urgell).

Pulitzer

ℹ Bergara 8
☎ 93 481 67 67
www.hotelpulitzer.es

One of the new generation of rinky dinky Barcelona hotels, the Pulitzer is a stylish dream in white tones with a beautiful roof terrace to boot. Walk in to a fabulously modern reception with Rococo details picked out, check out the salons with their white leather furniture and sky-high flower arrangements and then up to rooms which may not be huge but are super-sexy in design with whites and chocolates and caramels and suede. Every amenity you could want on holiday – and quite a few you probably won't bother with – is here (and they have a deal with Holmes Place if you're going to need a gym). All this just a short walk to the centre of the main gay drag and handy for the Ramblas and Paseo de Gracia. A real find.

Beauty and the Beach

ℹ Passeig Taulat 136 (5c)
☎ 93 266 05 62
www.beautyandthebeach.net
Ⓜ Metro: Poble Nou, bus 41

Beautiful B&B

If you're coming to Barcelona for a beach holiday, there's no better gay place to stay than this small and friendly bed and breakfast a few minutes' walk from the gay nudist strip, Mar Bella. And it's just a short bus hop to the Old City and La Rambla.

The three guest rooms at the top of a low-rise apartment block are plushly decorated in a contemporary palette, each with super-comfy queen-sized beds. The B&B is also fully airconditioned – a definite boon during a scorching summer night. There's a TV lounge for quiet evenings in, and a hifi wired into the bathroom so you can get in the mood for a night out while plucking your eyebrows. All guests can check their emails and surf the web using wide-band internet access. And if you give advance warning, your hosts – a charming gay couple, José María and Matt – will even cook for you. Blissful.

Centre of gay Sitges – Hotel Liberty

Hotel Liberty, Sitges

Illa de Cuba 45, Sitges

93 811 08 72 www.hotel-liberty-sitges.com

RENFE train: Sitges

Stepping out of Sitges station, the rainbow-striped sign outside Hotel Liberty is the first indication that you've arrived in a gay wonderland. And this is the must-stay place for gay boys and girls in town – though even non-guests are welcome to stop off and pick up Sitges maps and listings guides from reception.

A painstakingly renovated turn-of-the-century townhouse over five floors, its 12 high-ceilinged rooms match period stylings with modern conveniences and comforts. Each guestroom is airconditioned (though the stone floor helps keep things cool, too), and comes with satellite TV, minibar, phone and stereo system. Those facing the main road are triple-glazed – no chance of being woken by tipsy revellers staggering past – while those overlooking the gardens and pretty conservatory (where breakfast is served leisurely till midday) come with their own balconies and en suites.

The bar, with its relaxed, colonial feel, has a life of its own, hosting numerous local gay drinks parties, including a wildly popular girls' night. Located near the beach, bars and shops, Hotel Liberty is a gay idyll, and the multilingual staff work tirelessly to ensure a memorable stay.

Romantic by name...

AC DIPLOMATIC
ℹ️ C. Pau Clarís, 122
📞 93 272 38 10
Fax 93 272 38 11
www.achoteldiplomatic.com
Ⓜ️ Metro: Passeig de
Gràcia ● ③

One of Barcelona's
leading four-star
hotels, pitched
primarily at business
guests. But the
proximity to Gaudí's
major works, the
luxury shops on the
Passeig de Gràcia,
and the nearby bars
and clubs of the
Gaixample make it a
nifty bolt hole for
moneyed gay couples,
too.

HOTEL ACTUAL
ℹ️ C. Rosselló 238
(corner with Passeig de
Gràcia)
📞 93 552 05 50
Fax 93 552 05 55
www.hotelactual.com
Ⓜ️ Metro: Passeig de
Gràcia ● ②

Popular with the
trendy suits who do
business up on the A.
Diagonal, it's also
well-situated for the
gay scene tourist, a
short stroll from the
Gaixample bars.
Recently given a
sprightly facelift,
rooms are small, but
heavy on style: a
boutique feel on
a budget.

HOTEL CALIFORNIA
ℹ️ C. Rauric 14 (corner
with C. Fernando)
📞 93 317 77 66
Fax 93 317 54 74
www.hotelcaliforniabcn.com

Sleeping Around

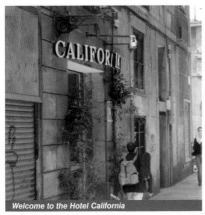

Welcome to the Hotel California

CHECKING IN

Metro: Liceu

Gay-friendly two-star in a decidedly ropey alley off the Barri Gòtic (centrally located, though). Forgive the slight shabbiness: the laid-back boho air is the main attraction.

HOSTAL BAIRES

C. Avinyó 37

Tel/fax 93 319 77 74

hostalbaires@terra.es

Metro: Jaume I,
Drassanes

Gay *hostal* set in a 17th-century palace in the Barri Gòtic, just five minutes from the Ramblas.

HOTEL GAUDÍ

C. Nou de la Rambla 12

93 317 90 32

Fax 93 412 26 36

www.hotelgaudi.es

Metro: Liceu

Just off La Rambla in the Raval district, this well-placed mid-range hotel's connection to Antonio Gaudí extends beyond just the name. There's a secret tunnel (closed to the public) linking it with his extraordinary mock medieval palace opposite, which was commissioned by his long-time patron Eusabe Güell. Take the Palau Güell tour for the full story (see p.34). Much of the grandiose palatial feel has stuck, and the public areas show strong nods to Gaudí's dreamy handiwork.

HOSTAL LAUSANNE

A. Puerta del Angel, 24 Plaça Catalunya

93 302 11 39, no fax

Metro: Catalunya

Well located on Barcelona's high-street shopping precinct, this gay-run (though not exclusively gay) two-star *hostal* opposite the El Corte Inglés has clean, functional rooms, with a large TV lounge and snack machine. Popular with young groups of backpacking friends.

HOTEL ORIENTE

La Rambla 45–47

93 302 25 58

Fax 93 412 38 19

www.husa.es

Metro: Drassanes

Reconstructed from a former monastery in 1842, this undisputed gem of the Barri Gòtic is now something of a museum piece. But the whiff of faded glamour only adds to the allure: Maria Callas would stay during her performances at the nearby Liceu opera house, and Errol Flynn holed up here in his heyday to escape adoring fans.

Fraying at the edges, the rooms are plain and perhaps a little pricey for a mid-range hotel on the Rambla. Still, it's perfect for enjoying the nightlife of the Barri Gòtic and the trendy Born district.

Faded glamour at the Oriente

TEDDY'S HOUSE

C. Roger de Llúria 104
93 458 71 40
teddyshouse@terra.es
Jaume I

Small, bear-friendly gay *hostal* in the Eixample.

GRAND HOTEL CENTRAL

Via Laietana, 30
93 295 79 00
www.grandhotelcentral.com

This new hotel really has got the lot, from its central location near the gothic cathedral to its pool on the roof, to the beautiful modern minimalist design of the place to the fact that it has some of the top eateries in town within its own four walls. Can be a bit on the pricey side, but if you're in the mood to splurge this is the place to do it in.

Sitges

ANTONIO'S

Passeig Vilanova 58
93 894 92 07
Fax 93 894 64 43
antonios_sitges@hotmail.com

Five attractive guestrooms – some with en suite – and just a few minutes' walk from the beach.

Open for the summer season only (May–October).

CALIPOLIS HOTEL

Passeig Marítim
93 894 15 00
Fax 93 894 07 64
www.hoteles-hesperia.es

A mixed four-star hotel, but popular with same-sex couples, as it faces the main gay beach. Check in for the queerest sea view in Sitges.

LA MASIA CASANOVA

Passatge Casanova 8
93 818 80 58
Canyelles

Slightly off the beaten track in nearby Canyelles and set against a formidable mountain backdrop, this converted (and recently renovated) farmhouse winery, some 11 kilometres out of town, is a luxury gay spot. There's a pool and bar, plus a great sauna, Jacuzzi and steam room. Minimum three days' stay.

HOTEL DE LA RENAIXENÇA

C. Illa de Cuba 13
93 894 83 75
Fax 93 894 81 67

Mixed gay-straight hotel pitched at the budget pocket. Rooms are small but clean, though the talking point is the lively bar, which has become a trendy meeting point for locals.

HOTEL ROMÀNTIC

C. Sant Isidre, 33
93 894 83 75
Fax 93 894 81 67
www.hotelromantic.com

Set in gorgeous ornamental gardens – complete with palms, vines and spouting fountains – the 55-room hotel occupies three 19th-century villas, and has retained its period charm. Perfect for lovers of outdoor dining is the garden restaurant, which, with its fantastic wine list and champagne cellar, is gourmet heaven.

The following price guides have been used for accommodation, per room per night

❶ = €10–€50
❷ = €50–€150
❸ = over €150

Panorama of the Plaça d'Espanya

Check This Out

These pages cover everything you need to know about getting to Barcelona. They tell you what to do to stay healthy, how to make the most of your money, and advise you about sex in the city. Find out when it's hot, when the parties are, and how generally to stay out of trouble.

Getting There

BY AIR

FLYING FROM THE UK

Regular flights to Barcelona's El Prat de Llobregat airport (BCN) depart from all major international airports, including London's main three. It is a fiercely competitive route, with low prices to be had on most carriers. The flight time from London is 1hr 45mins.

The most comfortable option is British Airways (www.ba.com, 0845 773 3377), which offers an extensive direct schedule every day from London Heathrow and London Gatwick, Manchester, Birmingham and Glasgow airports. Thanks to price slashing in recent years, BA can be better value than 'budget' rivals, with single flights from £39 (plus tax) and return tickets for around £100. Iberia (www.iberia.com) also operates from various UK airports.

Of the numerous 'no frills' airlines travelling to Barcelona, the market leader is EasyJet (www.easyjet.com). The airline operates most flights from London Luton, as well as London Gatwick, London Stansted, Liverpool, Glasgow, Bristol, Newcastle and East Midlands. BMIbaby (British Midland's budget airline, www.bmibaby.com) offers a 'no frills' service from East Midlands airport, and budget newcomer Jet2 (www.jet2.co.uk) flies from Leeds-Bradford.

The internet makes planning a trip to Barcelona simple. Try the following websites:

www.airfares.co.uk
www.cheapflights.co.uk
www.deckchair.com
www.dialflight.com
www.expedia.co.uk
www.flightbookers.com
www.opodo.co.uk
www.statravel.co.uk
www.flythomascook.com
www.travelocity.co.uk

Charter flight operators also fly to Barcelona from main and regional airports, with return flights starting at as little as £80.

Check out the travel classifieds of *Time Out* and *Loot*, or Teletext, for more details.

FLYING FROM NORTH AMERICA

Delta Airlines (www.delta.com) flies direct to Barcelona three times a day from New York. Iberia also operates a daily overnight service from Miami. Air Canada, Delta, Iberia and American Airlines all fly via Madrid, and have extensive travel networks using partnership airlines via other European capitals. It may prove more economical to fly into London Heathrow and fly onwards with a British carrier. (See p.131.)

The prices for indirect flights from North America to Barcelona range from $350 to $1,000. Try the following sites:

www.airbrokers.com
www.statravel.com
www.travelcuts.com
www.travelocity.com

FLYING FROM AUSTRALIA AND NEW ZEALAND

There are no direct flights to Spain from Australia and New Zealand, though Qantas (www.qantas.com.au) flies from both countries with a series of stopovers (usually London Heathrow).

ARRIVING IN BARCELONA

Barcelona's El Prat de Llobregat airport (93 298 38 38, www.barcelona-airport.com) is a convenient 13 kilometres (8 miles) south of the city. There are two main international terminals, A and B (C is for domestic routes). It is clean, orderly and with all the usual distractions: shop, cafés,

tourist information offices (open 9am– 5pm), cash machines and bureaux de change (open 7am–11pm). There are also left luggage lockers in Terminal B.

For up-to-the-minute information on flights to and from Barcelona, consult the airport website, www.barcelona-airport.com. The site also has weather forecasts – handy for last-minute packing adjustments.

GETTING FROM THE AIRPORT

AEROBUS
📞 906 427 017

A simple way to get into the city centre, the A1 Aerobus leaves directly outside terminal buildings A and B every 15 minutes between 6am and midnight. It takes about half an hour to Plaça de Catalunya, with stop-offs at Plaça d'Espanya and Gran Via de les Corts Catalanes. Returning to the airport, it leaves Plaça de Catalunya along C. d'Aragó (in the Gaixaimple), with pick-ups at Sants station and Plaça d'Espanya. The price is €3.60 one-way (*sencilla*) or €5.65 return (*ida y vuelta*), only available on the bus, so have change. The Aerobus is wheelchair accessible. Two local buses, 105 and 106, serve both airport terminals from Plaça d'Espana. They take longer but cost only €1 each way, and run later; the last 106 leaves the airport at 3.20am. Heading to the airport, the last 106 leaves Plaça d'Espanya at 3.50am. There is also a nightbus (*nitbus*) service to the airport, route EN, which picks up from Plaça de Catalunya, Plaça d'Espanya, and along Gran Via de les Corts Catalanes.

RENFE TRAIN

The RENFE train takes 20 mins to Barcelona Sants, 25 mins to Plaça de Catalunya, 27 mins to Arc de Triomf and 31 mins to El Clot-Aragó. Trains operate every 30 mins between 6.13am and 11.40pm, and cost €2 one-way. Returning to the airport, the train stops at Plaça de Catalunya every 8 and 38 mins past the hour. Beware works on the line during 2006 and 2007 which will cause delays and will mean you need to change trains to get into town.

TAXI

Expect to part with between €12 and €25 for a metered cab from outside the two main terminals, depending on traffic and where in the city you want to go. Fares are higher (by 10–20 per cent) after 10pm, and at weekends, and there is a 80¢ surcharge for each piece of luggage put in the boot. There is usually an abundance of taxis waiting so you shouldn't require the services of the taxi touts operating inside the terminal building.

ARRIVING BY BUS

It is possible to travel from London to Barcelona by bus, though the 24-hour journey will deter all but the most nervous of flyers. Eurolines (www.eurolines.com) offers single tickets from around £80, with returns from £110, though restricted Apex returns may be as little as £60.

Bussing into Barcelona is a more likely mode of transport for those already travelling in mainland Spain or neighbouring countries. Most long-distance buses come into the modern Estació d'Autobuses Barcelona-Nord (C Al Del 80, 93 265 65 08), a five-minute walk from

Tourist information

Arc de Triomf metro. Some services – including Eurolines – also stop at Sants station.

For those travelling on from Barcelona by bus, services are mostly operated out of Barcelona Nord – by Enatcar (93 245 88 56, www.enatcar.com) and its subsidiary, Alsa (902 422 242, www.alsa.es). During busy periods, it is advisable to book a seat at least 24 hours in advance.

ARRIVING BY TRAIN

Barcelona's main international and domestic station is Sants Estació, some 3 kilometres from Plaça de Catalunya, or a short metro journey (on the green L3 line). Sants is large, well equipped and unthreatening. Spain's state-run rail service is RENFE (902 24 02 02, www.renfe.es). For local journeys, use coins and euro notes in the ticket machines (which have optional instructions in English). Otherwise, there are tellers who often speak rudimentary English.

Some French services terminate at the impressive and underused 1920s Estació de Franca, close to Barceloneta metro.

ARRIVING BY SEA

Those considering a trip to Barcelona following a holiday on the Balearic island of Ibiza should consider the naval option. The Umafisa ferry (971 31 02 01, www.umafisa.com) docks at (and departs from) the Moll de Barcelona quay at the end of Avinguda Parel.lel. There's a 9-hour overnight sailing every day except Sunday, and prices range from €45.43 for lounge seating, and from €54 to €155.80 for a cabin, depending on facilities and occupancy.

Transmediterranea (93 295 91 34/35, www.southernferries.co.uk) operates regular services to and from Ibiza, with prices between €26.20 and €150.40. Both companies sail to Ibiza at night – but you can arrive in Barcelona from the island on a daytime sailing, perfect for topping up the tan.

ENTRY REQUIREMENTS

PASSPORTS AND VISAS

For trips of under three months, full passports are required by visitors from the UK, Ireland, Canada, USA, Australia and New Zealand. Citizens of the UK and Ireland planning to stay in Spain for more than this time need to obtain a residency permit (*permiso de residencia*) from the foreigners' office (*Oficina de Extranjeros*) at the Delegación del Gobierno (Avda Marques de Argentera 2, 93 482 05 60, metro Barceloneta, appointments 8am–3pm Mon–Fri). Non-EU nationals will need to obtain a visa in their own country prior to departure if they wish to stay for more than three months. As visa requirements frequently change, check with your Spanish Embassy if planning a long stay.

PEOPLE WITH HIV/AIDS

Spain has no specific restrictions on entry for people living with HIV/AIDS. Non-EU nationals applying for residency, work and student permits will be required to take a medical test. When travelling with anti-retroviral medication, ensure it is clearly labelled.

CUSTOMS

It is not usually necessary to make customs declarations if arriving from another EU country. You can bring in with you: 800 cigarettes or 400 cigarillos, 200 cigars or 1 kilo of loose tobacco, 10 litres of spirits (over 22 per cent alcohol), 20 litres of fortified wine or alcoholic drinks (under 22 per cent alcohol), plus 90 litres of wine and 110 litres of beer. Be warned that if you are carrying quantities this high, you could be asked to explain how it is all for personal use.

Non-EU residents can bring in 200 cigarettes or 100 cigarillos, 50 cigars or 250g of loose tobacco; plus one litre of spirits (over 22 per cent alcohol) or 2 litres of fortified wine or spirits under 22 per cent, plus 2 litres of wine and 50 grams of perfume. You'd be mad to, though.

Hop on and get around town

Alcohol in Spain beats duty free prices easily. Non-EU residents can claim back VAT (*IVA*) for purchases of over €90 – enquire at the airport on arrival or in the store as you buy.

In the city

TOURIST INFORMATION

Barcelona's well-staffed central tourist office on Plaça de Catalunya (906 30 12 82, www.barcelonaturisme.com) is open 9am–9pm daily. The English-speaking staff will supply you with free maps and information. You'll also find a hotel booking service (useful in an emergency, but you'll have to stand in very lengthy queues), bureau de change, souvenir shop and coin-operated internet access.

There are other tourist inform-ation offices in Sants station, open 8am–8pm (2pm closing at weekends in winter) and Plaça Jaume (10am–8pm, 10am–2pm weekends). In the summer, a mobile tourist information booth stands outside La Sagrada Família – look out for the red-jacketed information officers.

All tourist information offices are marked with a red sign with a white 'i' in the centre.

The city also offers a useful telephone information service, manned Mon–Sat, 9am–10pm. Dial 010 from any phone, and the operators will efficiently answer most queries you may have.

For those interested in exploring beyond Barcelona's city limits, there is a Turisme de Catalunya office in Palau Robert (Passeig de Gràcia 105, 93 238 40 00). Open 10am–7pm Mon–Sat, 10am–2pm Sunday.

ACCOMMODATION

Most hotels, hostels and guesthouses will display metropolitan attitudes towards same-sex couples. If at all worried, simply mention that you are gay when booking, but it shouldn't present a problem. Barcelona still has something of an accommodation crisis, so as a rule it is best to arrange somewhere to stay before arriving.

PUBLIC TRANSPORT

Barcelona is blessed with an efficient and integrated metro, train and bus network. The public transport website, www.tmb.net. is extremely useful. Not only can you search for public transport options on an address, area and even landmark, you can also click your starting point on a map, enter your destination, and it will provide you with a detailed description of the best way to get there, with journey times and any additional walking directions – all in English and printable.

METRO

The Barcelona metro is fast, clean and easy to use. It consists of five lines, easily identified by number and colour. At interchange points the signs state the final destination for trains stopping at each platform. A single journey costs €1.20, but the best option is usually a T-10 carnet which costs €6.65. This allows you ten trips, each with a free interchange onto any RENFE or FGC train, metro or bus within 1 hour 15 mins of validation. The same ticket can be used by more than one person, so one card will allow you and a partner or friend to take five trips together. Pass the ticket back over the gates once the first person has gone through.

There are also cards offering unlimited travel for €9.20 to €20 for between two and five days, and €42.75 for a month (T-Mes). These

Metro travel

insert it into the validation machine behind the driver. To ensure a bus stops, you need to flag it down as you would a taxi. Board at the front and get off at the middle or rear.

NIGHTBUS

Nightbuses (*nitbuses*) run on 16 urban routes 10.30pm–4am. They operate every 20–30 mins and most pass through Plaça de Catalunya, which is also the terminus for several services to areas further from the centre. Nightbuses work on the same pricing and ticketing system as daytime buses.

TRAINS

If heading out of Barcelona city centre, there is an extensive train network. RENFE and the FGC (www.fgc.net) run suburban trains and services to surrounding towns. For Sitges, take the train from Sants station. Fares vary depending on zones.

Travelling to Madrid from Sants, allow six to nine hours and expect to pay between €36 and €63 for standard class (*turista*), and up to €97 for first class (*preferente*). The Trenhotel operates an overnight service, the 'Antonio Gaudí', to the capital (www.renfe.es/empresa/glineas/glineas_hotel.html). A train to Valencia will take around five hours and cost between €29 and €33.50 turista.

TAXIS

Barcelona's taxis are yellow, black and plentiful – about 11,000 in total (most of them Skodas!). A taxi with

prices are for zone 1, which covers anywhere you'd reasonably want to go in the city, apart from the airport.

Cards can be bought from machines and ticket offices inside stations, lottery shops, the ServiCaixa ticket centres (which also sell gig, theatre and cinema tickets) and newspaper kiosks, but not on buses. Many new machines take credit and debit cards, but will require a PIN number for security.

You will only require your ticket to enter a station; there are few exit barriers, but hold on to it; fail to show a ticket on demand and you could face a €40 fine.

The Metro runs 5am–midnight Mon–Thur, 5am–2am Friday and Saturday, 6am–midnight Sunday.

BUS

Most bus routes operate 5am–10.30pm, with buses passing every 10–15 mins. Services become less frequent later in the evening and on Sundays. Only single journeys (€1.20) can be purchased on the bus; for multi-journey tickets valid on the buses, see 'Metro'. If you have a ticket like a T-Mes, simply an illuminated green light on the roof with a 'Lliure/Libre' sign in the window is for hire. Hail it as you would in any other city. Taxi ranks are located at major bus and train stations and other locations throughout the city centre.

The minimum fare is €2, and you will be charged extra for luggage and waiting time. Drivers may not carry more than €15 change; not many accept card payments. You shouldn't have difficulty finding an available taxi, or call or book online:

Fono-Taxi: 93 300 11 00
Radio-Taxi: 93 225 00 00
Radio Taxi '033': 933 033 033
Servi-Taxi: 933 300 300
For disabled-adapted taxi, call 93 481 1058 or 93 528 1111.

CAR HIRE

Hiring a car is a recommended option if travelling around Catalunya. Good public transport, bad parking and pleasant walking may put you off hiring if you are staying within the city. Drivers must be at least 21 years old (or up to 25 with some companies) and hold a valid driving licence. A credit card will be needed for the large deposit.

Europcar (www.europcar.com) has several depots across the city, at the airport, and in Sitges. Book in advance online. A compact car costs €300 for a week, or if you prefer racing through the Catalan countryside in style, convertibles start at €515.

EasyCar (www.easycar.com) has remarkably cheap car hire starting at €6 basic charge per day with depots at Sants station and Arc de Triomf in the centre.

In the heart of the Gaixample, try Avis (C. Casanova 209, 93 209 95 33) and Atesa/National (C.

Muntaner 45, 93 298 34 33). Both also have offices at the airport.

EMBASSIES

Embassies and Consulates are listed in the phone book under Consolats/Consulados. If calling outside office hours, most have an emergency contact number.

AUSTRALIA

Plaça Gal.la Placida, 1–3 First Floor (93 490 90 13 www.embaustralia.es). Metro Fontana. Buses 59, 70, 72. Open 10am–midday Mon–Fri. Closed August.

CANADA

C. Elisenda de Piños 10, Zona Alta (93 204 27 00, fax 93 204 27 01, www.canada-es.org). No metro, FGC train Reinda Elisenda. Buses 22, 64, 75. Open 10am–1pm Mon–Fri.

NEW ZEALAND

Travesera de Gràcia 64 (93 209 03 99, fax 93 202 08 90). Metro Passeig de Gràcia. Buses 22, 24, 48. Open Sept–June 9am–2pm and 4pm–7pm. Phone to check reduced hours in August.

REPUBLIC OF IRELAND

Gran Via Carlos III 94, Zona Alta (93 491 50 21, fax 93 411 29 21). Metro Maria Cristina or Les Corts. Buses 59, 70, 72. Open 10am–1pm Mon–Fri.

UNITED KINGDOM

Avinguda Diagonal 477, Eixample (93 366 62 00, fax 93 366 62 21, www.ukinspain.com). Metro Hospital Clínic. Buses 6, 7, 15, 33, 34. Open end of Sept–mid-June 9.30am–1.30pm, 4–5pm

All the sights are only a short bus ride away

Mon–Fri. Mid-June–mid-Sept 9am–2pm.

UNITED STATES

Passeig Reina Elisenda 23 (93 280 22 27, fax 93 205 52 06, www.embusa.es). No metro, FGC train Reina Elisenda. Buses 22, 64, 75. Open 9am–12.30pm and 3pm–5pm Mon–Fri.

POLICE

In terms of police attitudes towards gays, Catalonia is the most advanced area of Spain, and Barcelona's police forces are renowned for their metropolitan-mindedness.

If a crime is committed against you, report the incident as soon as possible to the local police force, the *Guardia Urbana*. You should go to the nearest police station (*comisaria*). You will need to fill in an official statement form (*denuncia*) which will be required for any insurance claims. It will be available in English. The most central *comisaria* is located at La Rambla 43 (93 344 13 00, metro Liceu or Drassanes, buses 14, 38, 59 or 91). Open 24 hours, it often has English-speaking officers on duty. At 7am–midnight Sun–Thur and 7am–2am Fri and Sat, you can go to the Turisme-Atenció at the same address – this office specialises in assisting tourists, and is particularly helpful with filling out *denuncias*.

To be connected to the nearest *comisaria*, call the Policia Nacional on 93 290 30 00.

Copy your passport and travel documents and leave them in your hotel – they will help considerably if the originals are lost or stolen. By law, you should carry some form of official ID, such as an identity card or passport.

In an emergency, call the Policia Nacional on 091.

For non-urgent matters, contact the Guardia Urbana on 192.

ATTITUDE TOWARDS GAY VISITORS

Gay men and lesbians are a crucial, visible part of Barcelona, so you should feel relaxed roaming the city. Attitudes become more conservative the further away from the city you travel, and you may find open signs of affection attract stares but rarely anything more threatening.

Remember, gay men in particular are often a target for petty, rather than hate, crime. Use common sense.

DRUGS

While drugs are widely available from scooter-riding sellers patrolling the streets of the Gaixample, all non-

Police presence

Meet at the fountains

prescription drugs are illegal. Cannabis is widely, and often openly, used, but it is still illegal to possess or consume in public places. Though the law permits smoking in private, you can still be arrested for possession.

SAFETY

Bag snatching and pickpocketing are common in Barcelona. It pays to take care along La Rambla, around the port and Barri Xinès at night, and in all crowded areas like the metro. Barcelonans party late so it's unlikely you'll ever be walking a main street alone at night. But if in doubt, take a taxi or nightbus. (See pp.136–137.)

Women should feel comfortable in most parts of the city. It is safe for women to walk in pairs in quiet areas at night, but single women should take a taxi.

HEALTH

Visitors to Barcelona can receive emergency medical treatment through the public health service – call 112 to be connected to an ambulance, or 061 direct. Several central hospitals, like the seafront Hospital del Mar, have casualty departments (*Urgéncies*). Phone 010 for information about your nearest hospital and medical practitioner.

EU nationals can get basic medical treatment for free with a European Health Insurance card. Non-EU nationals with private health insurance can receive state healthcare on a paying basis.

Don't expect gay bars and clubs to give away free condoms and lube. Most gay saunas – certainly those recommended in the *Working Out* section – hand out one condom on entry (though not always lube).

For travellers with HIV/AIDS, anti-retroviral medication comes under Spanish Social Security. To obtain extra supplies, a prescription is needed; some medications may have a different name and you would need to visit a doctor – therefore, it is advisable to bring enough medication for your stay.

The AIDS Information Line (900 21 22 22) has advice and information on local services from 9am–5.30pm Mon–Fri mid-Sept–May, 8am–3pm Mon–Fri June–mid-Sept.

GAY RESOURCES

Casal Lambda (C. Verdaguer i Callis 10, Barri Gòtic 93 319 55 50, www.lambdaweb.org, metro Urquinaona, buses 17,19,40,45) is a cultural centre and meeting point for gays and lesbians that has been supporting the local gay community and campaigning for gay rights since 1976. It is open 6–9pm Mon–Sat, often with social events at weekends. It is a good contact point for single travellers looking to be guided onto the local scene (their magazine *Lambda* has a useful listings section).

COMMUNICATION

TELEPHONES
Most payphones accept coins (minimum 2 cents), Telefónica phonecards and credit cards. A local call will cost about 15 cents, 50 cents to a mobile. Post offices, kiosks (*estancs*) and newsstands sell Telefónica phonecards.

Mobile phones (*móviles*) are now very popular in Barcelona. Rent a Phone allows you to rent mobile phones for the duration of your stay. They have a branch in the Gaixample (C. Numància 212, 93 280 21 31, www.rphone.es), and also at the Maremàgnum shopping mall at Port Vell (93 225 81 06).

To make an international call, dial 00 then the country code and the local area code (removing the first 0 for the UK) and number. The country codes are:

    Australia: 51
    Canada: 1
    New Zealand: 64
    Republic of Ireland: 353
    United Kingdom: 44
    United States: 1

INTERNATIONAL OPERATOR ASSISTANCE
Dial 1008 for Europe and North Africa, 1005 for the rest of the world. Most operators speak English. For International Directory enquiries, dial 025.

TO CALL BARCELONA
Dial your country's exit code (eg. 00 in the UK) then 34 for Spain. All local numbers in Barcelona have nine digits – if you see one with seven, put 93 in front of it. For National Directory Enquiries, dial 025 – usually operators will speak only Spanish and Catalan.

EMERGENCY NUMBERS
For emergency services, dial 112. The operator will connect you to the police (*policia*), fire service (*bomberos*), or ambulance services (*ambulancia*), as requested. Alternatively, dial:
Ambulance/*Ambulància:* 061
Fire Service/*Bombers*/*Bomberos:* 080
Policia Nacional: 092 (first choice for a police emergency).

INTERNET
Internet centres and cafés can be found all over Barcelona. The best place is easy Everything at La Rambla, 8 (www.easyeverything.com). Metro Drassanes or Liceu 8am–2.30am. Price of access depends on the time.

POST OFFICE
The main central post office, Correu Central (Plaça Antoni Lopez, 93 486 83 02, metro Jaume I or Barceloneta, buses 14, 17, 19, 36, 40, 45, 57, 59, 64, 157), is at the foot of the Barri Gòtic. Open 8.30am–9.30pm Mon–Sat, 9am–2pm Sun. Post boxes are yellow and marked Correos y Telégrafos. Collections are Monday to Friday only.

Barcelona is scattered with *estancs*/*estancos*, the traditional tobacco kiosks that also sell postage stamps, transport *targetes* and phonecards. They are marked with a brown and yellow sign and the word *tabac* or *tabacos*. Good for avoiding post office queues.

MONEY
Since 2002, Spain's official currency has been the euro. One euro (€) consists of 100 cents (¢), also referred to as centims in Catalan, centimos in Castillian. Euro notes come in denominations of 5, 10, 20,

CHECK THIS OUT

50, 100, 200 and 500, with coins of
1 and 2 euros.

Banks (*bancos*) will change
traveller's cheques and cash for a
commission. They won't change
personal cheques except those they
have issued. Banks are normally
open 8.30am–2pm Mon–Fri, and
8.30am–1pm Sat Oct–April only.
Savings banks (which offer the same
exchange services as normal banks)
are also open 4.30pm–7.45pm on
Thursdays Oct–May.

Foreign Exchange offices
(*cambios*) are generally open later –
7am–11pm in both terminals at the
airport; 8.30am–9.30pm in Sants
station and 8.30am–10pm Mon–Fri,
9am–5.30pm Sat–Sun in Barcelona
Nord bus station. Several *cambios*
along La Rambla remain open until
midnight, some as late as 3am
(July–Sept only). Some *cambios* don't
charge commission, but you'll find
their rate is probably lower.

The most convenient option is
using ATMs (*telebancos*), which are
very common and have instructions
in English. As they charge a
minimum fee, it makes sense to
withdraw larger amounts of cash.

In emergencies, the quickest way
to have money wired is Western
Union (Loterias Manuel Martin,
La Rambla 41, 93 412 70 14, metro
Liceu, buses 14, 38, 59, 91, open
9.30am–11pm Mon–Sat,
10am–midnight Sun).

In an emergency try the following numbers. All are open 24hrs and
have English-speaking operators:
American Express: 902 37 56 37

CREDIT CARD KEY
Amex = American Express
DC = Diners Club
M = MasterCard
V = Visa

Diners Club: 901 10 10 11
MasterCard: 900 97 12 31
Visa: 900 99 12 16.

TIPPING

Tips are appreciated but not always
expected. In a restaurant, leave
between five and ten per cent.
Some also leave a small tip for bar
staff, and it is normal to tip hotel
porters, chambermaids and
toilet/restroom attendants. As a
guide, tip a taxi driver five per cent
maximum of the fare, or more if
they have been particularly helpful.

EATING OUT

Catalans eat late. Restaurants open
around 1.30pm–4pm for lunch (the
main meal), and for dinner
9pm–11.30pm. In between meals,
take the edge off hunger with
a pastry and hot chocolate in
a *granja* bar.

Touristy restaurants have earlier
opening hours. Cafés and café bars
often open at 7am for breakfast and
can stay open until past midnight.
Bars tend to have a flurry from
7pm, but expect most to be quiet
until at least 10.30pm, then lively
until 3am. Clubs open around
midnight and keep going –
7am–9am on Saturday and Sunday.

OPENING HOURS

Generally, shops are open
9/10am–1/2pm and
4.30/5pm–8/9pm, though many do
not re-open in the afternoon on
Saturdays. Many department stores
and shopping centres stay open
10am–9pm Saturday, with some
open on Sunday.

Museums follow shop hours but
often reduce their hours in the
winter months. Most close on
Monday. Smaller museums can be
reluctant to apply a regular

Buy souvenirs with euros

timetable, so phone ahead.

ELECTRICITY

The standard current is 220V or
225AC. Australian, British, Irish and
New Zealand visitors can use two-
pin adaptor plugs, available in travel
shops and airports (or Barcelonan
department stores if you forget to
bring one). For standard Canadian
and US 110V appliances, a current
transformer will also be needed. A
few old buildings still use 125V. In
cheaper hotels, check before
plugging in your appliances.

CLIMATE

Barcelona has good weather all year
round. July and August are very hot,
though the sea breeze often prevents
it getting too humid. May, June and
early September have great warm
and sunny weather. October to
December is fresh, sometimes with
downpours (often in the evening).

SCENE

The Barcelona gay scene is big all
year round, with bars and clubs
reaching their capacity in the
summer months.

The gay scene in Sitges throbs
between June and early October,
while in the winter and spring it is
a relaxed and sleepy seaside town;
most gay bars and clubs are closed
but there is still a visible gay

presence, and February's Carnival
is huge.

Media

GAY PRESS

Most gay and some cultural venues
stock free gay publications like the
A3 style freesheet *Shangay*, its
pocket-sized spin-off, *Shanguide*,
and the slightly worthier *Lambda*
(www.lamdaweb.org). Trendy
free monthly *Nois*
(www.revistanois.com) has very
useful scene maps. For sheer
portability and clarity, you can't beat
Friends: The Gaymap, available
individually in Barcelona and Sitges,
and written in Spanish and English.
Available in most city-centre kiosks
is the gay men's monthly *Zero*
(www.zeropress.com), which likes
to hide its serious-minded content
behind sexy-model coverstars. It
also includes a handy pullout
Spanish scene guide,
Guía Zero.

GENERAL LISTINGS

Barcelona's ultimate listings guide is
gay-inclusive *Guía del Ocio*, available
at newsstands and kiosks
(www.guiadelociobcn.es). You may
also be handed a free copy of
Barcelona@Mas or *Metro* on the
metro, both good for listings.

TV AND RADIO

Barcelona's TV is rarely worth
staying in for. Radio stations in
Barcelona are abundant and Catalan
is prominent. BBC World Service
can be found on 15485 and 9195
KHz. Digital radio owners can also
listen to Barcelona's gay radio
station. See www.gaybarcelona.net
for details.

Useful phrases

Listed first in Spanish, then Catalan, with pronunciation in brackets

hello
hola (oh-la) / hola (oh-la)

goodbye
adios (ah-dee-yoss) / adéu (ah-DEY-yoo)

good morning
buenas dias (bwen-as dee-yas) / bon dia (bon DEE-ya)

good afternoon
buenas tardes (bwen-as tar-des) / bona tarda (boh-na tar-da)

goodnight
buenas noches (bwen-as noh-chess) / bona nit (boh-na neet)

please
por favor (por FAH-vor) / si us plau (syoos-plow)

thank you (very much)
(muchas) gracias (moo-chas gra-see-yas) / moltes gràcies (moll gra-syes)

More expressions in Spanish and Catalan

I don't speak Spanish / Catalan
no hablo castellano / catalàn
no parlo castellà / català

do you speak English?
¿habla inglés? / ¿parla anglès?

I don't understand
no entiendo / no l'entenc

speak more slowly, please
hable más despacio, por favor
pot parlar més poc a poc, si us plau

excuse me (for attention)
oiga / escolti

I'm sorry
perdón / perdoni

OK
vale / molt bé

yes – sí
no – no

Asking directions in Spanish

do you know the way to…?
sabe cómo llegar a…/ para ir a…?

train – tren
ticket – un billete
single ticket – billete sencillo

return – ida y vuelta
next stop – la próxima parada
how much is it?
cuánto es?

Booking a room in Spanish

do you have a double / single for tonight / three days / one week?
tiene una habitación doble / para una persona para esta noche / tres dias / una semana?

I / we have a reservation
tengo / tenemos reserva
with / without bathroom / shower – con / sin / baño / ducha
double bed – cama doble
twin beds – con dos camas
breakfast included – desayuno incluido

Numbers

1 – un / uno / una
2 – dos
3 – tres
4 – cuatro
5 – cinco
6 – seis
7 – siete
8 – ocho
9 – nueve
10 – diez

11 – once
12 – doce
13 – trece
14 – catorce
15 – quinze
16 – dieciséis
17 – diecisiete
18 – dieciocho
19 – diecinueve
20 – veinte
21 – veintiuno
22 – veintidos
25 – veinitcinco
30 – treinta
40 – cuarenta
50 – cincuenta
60 – sesenta
70 – setenta
80 – ochenta
90 – noventa
100 – cien
200 – doscientos
253 – doscientos cincuenta y tres
1000 – mil
2000 – dos mil
1,000,000 – un millión

Days and Dates

Monday – Lunes
Tuesday – Martes
Wednesday – Miércoles
Thursday – Jueves
Friday – Viernes
Saturday – Sábado
Sunday – Domingo

January – Enero
February – Febrero
March – Marzo
April – Abril
May – Mayo
June – Junio
July – Julio
August – Agosto

September – Septiembre
October – Octubre
November – Noviembre
December – Diciembre

Meeting People

what's your name?
cómo se llama?

my name is…
me llamo…

where are you from?
de dónde eres?

I'm Australian / Canadian / English / Irish / from New Zealand / from the USA
soy australiano / a / canadiense / inglés/esa irlandés / esa de Nueva Zelanda, estadounidense

NB – to some, American (americano / a) applies to North, South and Central America.

would you like a drink?
quiere beber algo?

would you like to dance?
quieres bailar?

you're very handsome / pretty (for girl)
– eres muy guapo / a

can I take you to dinner?
te gustaría cenar conmigo?

here's my number
– este es mi número

I have a boyfriend / girlfriend / partner – tengo novio/novia/pareja

do you have a condom? tienes un condón?

come and visit me in…
ven a verme en…

you made my stay in Barcelona very special –
hiciste mi estancía en Barcelona muy especial

INDEX

INDEX

NOTEBOOK

out AROUND **NOTEBOOK**

out AROUND

Name _____

Address _____

_____

_____

Tel _____

Fax _____

email _____

Name _____

Address _____

_____

_____

Tel _____

Fax _____

email _____

Name _____

Address _____

_____

_____

Tel _____

Fax _____

email _____

Name _____

Address _____

_____

_____

Tel _____

Fax _____

email _____

Name _____

Address _____

_____

_____

Tel _____

Fax _____

email _____

Name _____

Address _____

_____

_____

Tel _____

Fax _____

email _____

out AROUND **CONTACT LIST**

Name _____

Address _____

_____

_____

Tel _____

Fax _____

email _____

Name _____

Address _____

_____

_____

Tel _____

Fax _____

email _____

Name _____

Address _____

_____

_____

Tel _____

Fax _____

email _____

Name _____

Address _____

_____

_____

Tel _____

Fax _____

email _____

Name _____

Address _____

_____

_____

Tel _____

Fax _____

email _____

Name _____

Address _____

_____

_____

Tel _____

Fax _____

email _____

CONTACT LIST out AROUND

Name _____

Address _____

_____

_____

Tel _____

Fax _____

email _____

Name _____

Address _____

_____

_____

Tel _____

Fax _____

email _____

Name _____

Address _____

_____

_____

Tel _____

Fax _____

email _____

Name _____

Address _____

_____

_____

Tel _____

Fax _____

email _____

Name _____

Address _____

_____

_____

Tel _____

Fax _____

email _____

Name _____

Address _____

_____

_____

Tel _____

Fax _____

email _____

MY TOP RESTAURANTS

My Top Restaurants

Restaurant _____

Contact Details _____

_____

Comments _____

_____

_____

_____

Restaurant _____

Contact Details _____

_____

Comments _____

_____

_____

_____

Restaurant _____

Contact Details _____

_____

Comments _____

_____

_____

_____

My Top Bars

Bar

Contact Details

Comments

Bar

Contact Details

Comments

Bar

Contact Details

Comments

MY TOP CLUBS

My Top Clubs

Club _____

Contact Details _____

_____

Comments _____

_____

_____

_____

Club _____

Contact Details _____

_____

Comments _____

_____

_____

_____

Club _____

Contact Details _____

_____

Comments _____

_____

_____

_____

If you enjoyed using this book, or even if you didn't, you can help us to improve future editions by letting us have your feedback. Maybe you've made a great discovery on your travels that we don't already feature, perhaps you'd like to inform us about recent changes to anything that we do include, or you simply want to let us know your thoughts about this guidebook and how we can make it even better. Please take a moment to complete this form and return it to the address overleaf, or send your thoughts to books@thomascook.com

As an extra 'thank you' from Thomas Cook Publishing, you'll be automatically entered into our exciting monthly prize draw.

Feedback Form

1 Which Out Around guide did you purchase?

2 Have you purchased other Out Around guides in the series?

☐ Yes ☐ No   If Yes, please specify

3 Which of the following tempted you into buying your Out Around guide. (Please tick as appropriate)

☐ The cover
☐ The price
☐ The rainbow device
☐ The fact it was a dedicated gay travel guide
☐ Other

4 Please rate the following features of your 'Out Around guide' for their value to you (circle VU for 'very useful', U for 'useful', NU for 'little or no use')

'A Day Out' features	VU	U	NU
Top Sights	VU	U	NU
Top restaurants and cafés and listings	VU	U	NU
Top shops and listings	VU	U	NU
Top hotels and listings	VU	U	NU
Top clubs and bars and listings	VU	U	NU
Theatre and music venues	VU	U	NU
Gyms and sauna choices	VU	U	NU
Practical information	VU	U	NU

FEEDBACK FORM

Feedback Form

5 How did you book your holiday?

☐ Package deal
☐ Package deal through a gay-specific tour operator
☐ Flight only
☐ Accommodation only
☐ Flight and accommodation booked separately

6 How many people are travelling in your party?

7 Which other cities do you intend to/have travelled to in the next/past 12 months?

Amsterdam	Yes ☐	No ☐
Barcelona and Sitges	Yes ☐	No ☐
Berlin	Yes ☐	No ☐
London	Yes ☐	No ☐
Miami	Yes ☐	No ☐
New York	Yes ☐	No ☐
Paris	Yes ☐	No ☐
San Francisco	Yes ☐	No ☐
Sydney	Yes ☐	No ☐

Other (please specify)

8 Please tell us about any features that in your opinion could be changed, improved, or added in future editions of the book, or any other comments you would like to make concerning the book:

9 Your age category
☐ under 21 ☐ 21-30 ☐ 31-40 ☐ 41-50 ☐ 51+

**Please detach or photocopy this page and send it to:
The Editor,
Thomas Cook Publishing,
PO Box 227
Coningsby Road
Peterborough
PE3 8SB
UK**

First name (or initials)

Last name

Your full address (Please include postal or zip code)

Your daytime telephone number: